RAIN
FORESTS

Other Books in the At Issue Series:

RAIN FORESTS

HaiSong Harvey, *Book Editor*

Daniel Leone, *Publisher*
Bonnie Szumski, *Editorial Director*
Scott Barbour, *Managing Editor*

An Opposing Viewpoints® Series

Greenhaven Press, Inc.
San Diego, California

Library of Congress Cataloging-in-Publication Data

Rain forests / HaiSong Harvey, book editor.
        p. cm. — (At issue)
    Includes bibliographical references and index.
    ISBN 0-7377-0804-2 (pbk. : alk. paper) —
ISBN 0-7377-0805-0 (lib. : alk. paper)
    1. Rain forest conservation. I. Harvey, HaiSong. II. At issue
(San Diego, Calif.)

SD411 .R33   2002
333.75'16—dc21   2001023903
                                                              CIP

© 2002 by Greenhaven Press, Inc., PO Box 289009,
San Diego, CA 92198-9009

Printed in the U.S.A.

Table of Contents

Introduction

Although rain forests are located in both tropical and temperate climate zones, most of the world's rain forests lie in the equatorial regions of South America, West Africa, and Southeast Asia, forming a lush green belt around the planet. The world's largest rain forest is found in the Amazon River Basin in South America and is 5.2 square kilometers in size. Rain forests receive between 160 and 400 inches of rain annually and have an average temperature of 80 degrees Fahrenheit. Due to this extreme moisture and warmth, the forests teem with life. Occupying only 6 to 7 percent of the planet's land surface, they are home to more than half of the world's plant and animal species.

In recent years, a great deal of concern has arisen over the destruction of the forests. Environmentalists warn that over one-half of the earth's original rain forests have been wiped out. According to the Rainforest Alliance, a forest conservation organization, the world's tropical forests have shrunk from 7.1 billion acres in 1800 to 3.5 billion acres at present. "We're losing 33.8 million acres of tropical forest per year," the alliance reports, "more than the total area of New Hampshire, Vermont, Massachusetts, Rhode Island, Connecticut, New Jersey, and Delaware combined—2.8 million acres lost per month . . . 93,000 acres/day . . . 3,800 acres/hour . . . 64 acres/minute." The primary causes of forest destruction are commercial logging, mining operations, and slashing and burning by local farmers to clear land for growing crops and grazing livestock.

This destruction of the rain forests concerns environmentalists for several reasons. Tropical rain forests contain about 45 percent of the world's plant species. According to some estimates, up to thirty thousand of these species have yet to be identified. Destroying the forests could cause the extinction of many plants—as well as the animals that depend on them—thus threatening the planet's biodiversity. In addition, many of these plants may prove valuable as medicines. According to the National Cancer Institute, 70 percent of the plants that are useful for treating cancer come from the rain forests. Drugs used to treat other illnesses are found there as well. Scientists fear that destroying the rain forests threatens to wipe out entire species of plants before their value as medicine can be determined.

Rain forests also function as "carbon sinks" because they hold reserves of carbon in their vegetation. When the forests are destroyed, they release carbon into the atmosphere in the form of carbon dioxide (CO_2), a gas that contributes to global warming. The United Nations estimates that clearing of the rain forests is responsible for 20 percent of atmospheric CO_2, making deforestation a major contributor to global warming.

A more direct consequence of tropical deforestation involves the displacement of indigenous peoples and entire communities. Encroachment by loggers, farmers, and miners has forced many indigenous inhabitants to abandon their homes and lands. Not only have millions of forest acres been denuded, but thousands of miles of roads have been constructed, increasing expansion into indigenous peoples' unspoiled territory. According to the Rainforest Alliance, over ninety Amazonian tribes are believed to have disappeared in the twentieth century.

While environmentalists decry these developments, some scientists debate the extent of tropical deforestation. Critics contend that environmentalists vastly overestimate the amount of deforestation. For example, environmentalists produce conflicting estimates of the amount of forest being destroyed, with estimates ranging from the equivalent of two football fields being leveled every second to twenty football fields being denuded every minute. Some believe that this inconsistency makes the claims of environmentalists suspect. According to Patrick Moore, a founding member of the environmental organization Greenpeace, by some accounts, humanity "would have cleared 50 times the size of the Amazon already." In actuality, Moore states, satellite data reviewed by the National Institute for Research in Amazonia reveals that 87.5 percent of the Amazonian rain forest remains standing. Furthermore, of the 12.5 percent that has been cleared, up to one-half is regrowing. Therefore, Moore insists, "The Amazon rainforest is more than 90 percent intact."

Others debate the threat that deforestation poses to biodiversity, global climate, and indigenous people. Philip Stott, a professor of biogeography, is an especially strong critic of the environmentalist perspective on these issues. He insists that predictions of species extinction are based on computer models that have "no scientific basis." Stott also dismisses the claim that the forests are "carbon sinks." Due to the natural decomposition process, he argues, rain forests actually produce more CO_2 than they absorb. Stott concludes that the public's concern over rain forests has been encouraged by various myths designed

> to persuade us that the rain forest is vital for maintaining the stability and balance of the Earth—for our very own survival on this planet. Are the forests not "the lungs of the Earth"? "The living sinks" that will help to buffer our human excesses of carbon dioxide emissions as we recklessly warm the atmosphere? The richest remaining "library" of genetic resources for us to store, read, and use? "The last refuge" of forest people living in harmony in an untainted Golden Age and Garden of Eden? . . . It is all nonsense.

Whether the threat of deforestation is nonsense is one of the issues debated in *At Issue: Rain Forests*. Contributors to this anthology examine the extent of deforestation, the forces that threaten the rain forests, and various conservation efforts. Throughout these selections, authors consider the fate of some of the most majestic natural environments on the planet. These issues are certain to provoke ongoing controversy as environmentalists continue to characterize the protection of the rain forests as essential to the survival of humanity. As stated by the Rainforest Alliance, "The future of over 50% of Earth's plants and animals—and hundreds of human cultures—will be determined within the next few decades. Since our lives are so dependent on the forest's bounty, our future is at stake as well."

1

The Amazon Rain Forest Is in Danger of Being Destroyed

Devadas Vittal

Devadas Vittal is a student of political science and international studies at American University in Washington, D.C.

The destruction of the Amazon rain forest has continued even as governments and environmental groups have been trying to slow it down for years. Saving the Amazon rain forest is vitally important for many reasons. First, 25 percent of the pharmaceuticals consumed in the United States are derived from plants in the rain forest. The Amazon rain forest plays a significant role in global weather patterns. Finally, the Amazon rain forest is home to thousands of species of plants, animals, and birds: Destroying the forest means destroying the wildlife. The threats to the Amazon are numerous and include commercial logging, urbanization, and multinational corporations. However, some progress is being made in the battle to save the Amazon rain forest. In April 1998, a new initiative established a protected area of 25 million hectares (62 million acres), with plans to increase this protected area in the future.

We have all been hearing about the destruction of the Amazonian rainforest for years. For roughly the same amount of time, various governmental entities and NGOs (Non-governmental organizations) have employed activism and various other strategies to try to stop or slow down the rate of rainforest destruction. The battle to save the Amazonian rainforest may seem like a hopeless cause. The NGOs such as Rainforest Action Network have taken direct approaches such as protests, boycotts, and lobbying on Capitol Hill for "rainforest friendly" legislation. While the decades of hard work on the part of these NGOs have made significant gains, the destruction still continues. If this deforestation is to stop, a greater effort must be made to understand the root causes behind the destruction of the Amazonian rainforest. Only then can comprehensive

Reprinted from Devadas Vittal, Introduction: *What Is the Amazon Rainforest?* Internet: http://www.homepages.go.com/homepages/d/v/i/dvittal/amazon/intro.html, November 1999, by permission of the author.

efforts be made to stop the cutting down of one of the world's most delicate natural resources.

The social factors are many and complex. The institutional factors are myriad. We have heard a lot about saving the rainforest, but few people outside the scientific community really understand why a group of trees in South America are important to them. Fewer still realize the social, and eventually economic, costs that will accrue between now and when the rainforest of Amazonia is wiped from the face of the earth.

What is the Amazonian rainforest?

The Amazonian Tropical Rainforest is an area of the South American continent that covers parts of five countries. Included under this umbrella are parts of Brazil, Venezuela, Colombia, Ecuador, and Peru. Hence it is not inconceivable that changing the fundamental type of ecosystem of an area this large will have potentially global consequences. The area defined as the Amazonian rainforest covers 914 million acres according to World Bank and World Wildlife Fund statistics.[1]

The rainforest, because of its sheer size, is a self sustaining climate system. The rainforest creates its own weather patterns. It's not called the rainforest for nothing. Water that evaporates from one part of the rainforest eventually triggers rain on another part of the rainforest. If a large part of the periphery of the rainforest is cut down, that area dries up, becomes overgrown with brush and weeds, and ceases to be part of the system. And because the entire system is interconnected, there is a critical mass needed for the system to continue to be viable. If less than the critical mass remains, the climate patterns will probably shift enough to eliminate most of the rainfall for the rest of the system, thus putting the entire rainforest in jeopardy.

Why should anyone care about the rainforest?

The rainforest is one of the oldest[2] and most diverse ecosystems in the world. Very few ecosystem biomes that were in existence during the time of the dinosaurs still exist today, but scientists say that the rainforests is one of them.[3] This large expanse of time has allowed animals and plants to evolve into an astonishing array of flora and fauna of every color, shape, size, texture, and genetic sequence.

25% of the pharmaceuticals consumed in the United States came from plants in the rainforest.[4] Because the vast majority of the Amazon rainforest has not been catalogued, the exact number of species in the Amazon rainforest is unknown. The World Bank estimates that 10% of all the world's species live in the Brazilian Amazon and most of them are found only in that area.[5] The NGO Greenpeace puts the percentage of the world's species in the rainforest at an astonishing 50%.[6] Experts also disagree on exactly how many species will become extinct due to the deforestation. It is unfortunate because many of these plants and animal species which will be lost forever to deforestation might have produced cures for diseases such as cancer and AIDS. Quinine, the only medicine effective against malaria, was only found in the Cinchona tree of South America until synthetics were derived.[7] However original quinine is still necessary since some strains of malaria have developed resistance to the synthetic version.[8] Cures to many other diseases have yet to be found in the rainforest, but because of species extinction, they may remain hidden forever.

It is a widely accepted estimate among many biologists that we are losing as many as 137 species per day to all causes,[9] including habitat loss. Pharmaceutical companies are rushing to analyze as many plants and animals as they can for medicinal value before these species disappear forever.

The rainforest provides us with several products we may not even realize come from the rainforest. Some ingredients for products which we in the developed world use everyday such as soaps, mouthwashes, shampoos, food coloring, and food preservatives come directly from the plants which grow only in rainforests. Rubber is produced from latex, which is gleaned from a tree that grows only in the rainforest. Lately, synthetic rubber has decreased our dependence on the rainforest for rubber, however. Many nuts and fruits were the reason that native peoples were able to live in the rainforest for thousands of years. The rainforest now provides a sustainable source of living and food for hundreds of thousands of native peoples.

The Amazon rainforest converts about 1 trillion pounds of carbon dioxide into oxygen through photosynthesis.[10] It is for this reason that the Brazilian Amazon is called "the Earth's Lungs." Almost all of that oxygen is consumed by bacteria in the soil which break down dead material and detritus, however.[11]

25% of the pharmaceuticals consumed in the United States came from plants in the rainforest.

Not only do trees in the Amazon absorb carbon dioxide but they also absorb the sun's excess energy that might otherwise go towards fueling storms. We are only beginning to understand the meteorological implications of replacing green space with asphalt and dirt. For example, a NASA study of 25 years of weather observations in the greater Atlanta area revealed that the region's explosive rate of development was having a significant impact on weather patterns.[12] Severe thunderstorms should normally occur in the evening after the sun has energized the atmosphere and heated the land. A thunderstorm is classified as severe not because of how much rain it has, but by how much energy it expends, the threshold being the production of hail more than ¾ of an inch in diameter or winds in excess of 57 mph. The idea is that more energy in a storm causes a greater risk of injury or damage. Longtime residents of Atlanta had said that they were noticing more early morning severe thunderstorms and rainstorms that lasted until noon.[13] The asphalt which is replacing vegetation around Atlanta stores the heat of the sun and releases it at night, making it just as warm at night as it is during the day. Thus, severe thunderstorms that should only occur after a long hot day are also occurring during the normally cool early morning hours, with greater frequency and intensity. The deforestation and urbanization trend appears to be what is going on in the Amazon Basin, but on a much larger scale. The problem is that we don't know what effect the deforestation of an area the size of the Amazon Basin will have on the world's weather patterns.

The Amazon has connections with far removed weather systems, most of which we still do not understand or even know about. For instance, a few years ago, it was discovered that most of the soil in the Amazon region did not come from South America, but rather from the African Sahara desert. It was revealed that this relationship has been sustaining the rainforest for thousands of years with new minerals carried on the winds from Africa.

The politics and economics of rainforest destruction

There are many reasons behind the destruction of the rainforest and to fully understand what is happening, we must consider all of them together. One of the most noteworthy causes of this has been the demand for rainforest wood in some of the more developed countries. The hardwoods that come only from the large trees which grow in the rainforest are in high demand in the more developed countries. A visit to your local furniture store will illustrate this point adequately. In the rainforest, mahogany, teak, and rosewood have natural water-resistant properties that keep them from rotting. This trait translates into high demand by consumers in the United States and Japan.[14] These trees are turned into wood chips, furniture, caskets, and toothpicks.[15] Right now, Japan is the largest consumer of rainforest wood, followed by the United States.[16] The World Wildlife Fund estimates that the United States consumes 60% of all mahogany that is harvested.[17, 18] The demand for wood and resultant opportunities for cashing in have caused some timber companies to use heavy-handed tactics with indigenous peoples who want to preserve their sections of the rainforest. Brazil has laws set up to protect the rights of indigenous peoples. However, in 1995, the Brazilian government had to intervene in armed fighting between gunmen for the Sudoeste Timber Company and the Xikrin Kayapo Indians.[19] This incident is certainly not unique. Reports in the local Brazilian media say that gunmen hired by logging companies have assassinated eight members of indigenous groups who had tried to defend their land from loggers.[20] Native peoples continue to fight off armed incursions by logging and mining companies who illegally harvest land that has been set aside for use by native peoples.

The largest cause of rainforest destruction is urbanization on a massive scale.[21] The trend toward the urbanization of Amazonia started out after World War II.[22] In 1964, a new authoritarian government looked toward the west in alarm at a vast region that was essentially "uninhabited," which they saw as a threat to their national security.[23] In 1960 this sentiment was embodied by the writings of a famous Brazilian politician and historian, A.C.F. Reis, who constantly warned about the perceived avarice of other countries towards the Amazon region.[24] The military leaders of Brazil wanted to speed up the settlement of the Amazon region to protect against possible invasion.[25] The Amazon fever was further fed by a report by the United Nations Food and Agricultural Organization in 1971 that implied that the Amazon region, if it were "intensively farmed," could provide food for up to 36 million people.[26] Although we now know that there were some serious flaws in the report, at the time the report was seen as another reason for pursuing an aggressive settlement and urbanization program in the Amazon.

During this time, most of the inhabitants of Brazil were landless peasants who lived and worked on "minifundios" or "latifundios." These minifundios and latifundios are plantation-like arrangements where the land is owned by one person or a family and peasants are employed in the farming of the land, often not earning enough money to feed themselves. The land tenure system in Brazil is such that most of the land is concentrated in the hands of the few. Moreover, as is always the case in situations where political power is inequitably distributed, land reform is made almost impossible by the fact that most of the political power is concentrated in the hands of the rich. Since most of the land is concentrated in the hands of the rich, there is little land to be distributed to the landless poor. Hence, the colonization of the rainforest interior in the post-WWII period had been seen as achieving two goals: consolidating the government's power over its own territory, and also helping alleviate hunger and poverty by providing landless and dispossessed peasants with land to farm.[27]

A few years ago, it was discovered that most of the soil in the Amazon region did not come from South America, but rather from the African Sahara desert.

The peasants who worked on the minifundios and latifundios often walked the fine line between having enough to eat and dying of starvation. It is a widely accepted tenet of social science that peasants are extremely risk averse. When presented with the opportunity to migrate, many of the peasants were reluctant considering that their lives were at risk if the promises of a fertile plot of arable land turned out to be false. However, the government initiated a massive marketing campaign on the radio, on television and in the newspapers.[28] The government flew some settlers to government outposts in the Brazilian rainforest states of Acre and Rondonia in "chartered jets and air force transport planes."[29] The government launched a massive road building campaign to sustain the new settlements in the rainforest with new settlers. The first highway through the rainforest was completed in 1964 connecting Belem with the capital, Brasilia.[30] In 1970 General Emilio Medíci, who was head of government at the time, proposed building 15,000 kilometers of highways in the Amazon region.[31, 32] This system of "National Integration Highways," similar to our interstate highway system, was envisioned by the country's military leaders connecting every part of the country and consolidating their power over the country further.[33,34]

It can be argued that there are some parallels between the settlement of the Amazon region in Brazil after WWII and the settlement of the trans-Appalachian region in the United States after the revolutionary war. Both countries looked towards the west at a vast region that belonged to them on paper yet was not "settled." Both countries seemed to fear other countries trying to invade and take over their territory. Both countries built roads through the forest to facilitate settlement and integration. And both countries *thought* that the lands were fertile enough to support millions of new settlers. However, the parallels end there.

There were a few things that nobody knew or took into account when this massive colonization program in Brazil began in the 1960s. Initially, those who were farming the Amazon Basin were achieving very good crop yields; but after farming the same land more than once, the crop yields dropped dramatically. The land on which the rainforest sits is extremely infertile. The soil a few inches deep is extremely sandy and is not nutrient rich. In general, crops can only be grown once or twice. After that, heavy usage of fertilizers is required. For poor farmers, this is usually not an option. They simply move on and cut down a new section of rainforest. When the rainforest is cut down, it ceases to be part of the forest ecosystem and climate system. That area of land no longer receives rain and nutrients from the rest of the system.

Initially, the World Bank, which had funded the most recent phase of Amazonian settlement in a scheme called the "polonoroeste project," discounted the arguments of those who said that the Amazon region could not sustain so many farmers. However, the World Bank acknowledges now that it may have made a mistake in financing the mass migration. The findings of a World Bank book, *Sustainable Settlement in the Amazon*, now say that much of the Amazonian frontier land cleared by pioneers in the 1970s had become "agriculturally unproductive."[35] Finding that the land could no longer sustain them, many peasants flooded back to the cities in the 1980s contributing further to the poverty problem in Brazil, which is where Brazil now finds itself.

In Southwestern Brazil, recently massive oil and natural gas reserves were discovered in an area straddling the Peruvian-Brazilian border. Migrants and multinational companies flocked to the area. In the Brazilian states of Acre and Rondonia, oil, natural gas, and metal ores such as gold have also been discovered.[36] These reserves are being developed, which will fuel further development and attract more companies to the area. It is estimated that approximately 200,000 independent gold miners were operating in the Amazon region in 1990.[37]

Mahogany, teak, and rosewood have been in high demand by consumers in the United States and Japan for their natural water-resistant properties.

The multinational corporations operating in the Amazon rainforest have also been the reason for much destruction and the target of many protests and much criticism. Since the end of World War II the Brazilian government has seen the Amazon as an area to be exploited for its timber and now for its underground riches. With this, they invited several transnational companies to set up shop in the Amazon. Between 1966 and 1970, the government's "Operation Amazonia" granted companies exemptions from corporate income taxes for ten to fifteen years as long as they invested in ventures in the new Amazonian frontier.[38] Tariffs were lowered for companies bringing in materials needed for the development of the Amazonian frontier.[39] Today as a result of the Brazilian government's heavy external debt, which totaled almost $220 billion in the year 2000,[40] the Amazonian frontier remains opened directly for exploitation by any company that is willing to make the investment and provide tax revenue to a government in desperate need of cash.

Among the companies trying to profit from activities that destroy the Amazon rainforest are several that are household names in the U.S. and Japan. These include banks, paper, timber, chemical, and oil companies. The charges of damaging activities leveled at multinational corporations include supplying bulldozers and logging trucks, manufacturing and selling paper and lumber made from rainforest and old-growth forest wood, mining under the rainforest, trading and importing rainforest wood, drilling for oil in the Amazon Basin, and U.S. and Japanese banks' financing these projects.[41] Rainforest Action Network leads boycotts of these companies and tries to educate consumers about corporate activities. Several of these boycotts and public education campaigns have yielded very positive results.

While political and economic factors cannot be ignored, from the environmental NGOs' past victories, it is quite apparent that consumers acting collectively can leverage a considerable amount of power in the short term in influencing whether companies leave footprints on the natural world or whether they leave craters.

Hope for the future

Some progress is beginning to be made in the battle to save the Amazonian rainforest. Brazil is beginning to remove itself from under the yolk of external debt. The amount of external debt owed by the Brazilian government, while still considerable, has finally posted a decline in the year 2000 after several straight years of increase.[42]

Certain actions have signaled that the World Bank has finally realized the value of the Amazon rainforest, if not rainforests elsewhere in the world. In 1995, former Brazilian President Jose Sarney signed into law a bill which protects about 5 million acres as extractive reserves for people such as rubber tappers, nut and fruit gatherers and others who make their livelihood from sustainable uses of the rainforest.[43] In April 1998, a new initiative announced by President Fernando Cardoso, under pressure and in partnership with the World Bank, established a protected area of 62 million acres.[44] The World Bank in an alliance with the World Wildlife Fund has committed itself to increasing the protected area of the Amazon from 3.49% to protecting at least 10% of the Amazon rainforest by the year 2000.[45] However, the best news of all may be that the people and the environment do not necessarily have to be at cross-purposes, for several reasons. Common sense tells us that a stand of trees that is providing fruits, nuts, and other products is almost certainly more economically valuable over the long term than an infertile plot of land that has become overgrown with weeds. In addition, pharmaceutical company royalties from new drugs may become a valuable source of government revenue, perhaps supplanting tax revenue from destructive mining activities, if such a program is administered properly. And eco-tourism can serve to infuse much needed capital into communities that lack it. Ironically, the economic value that now threatens the rainforest may ultimately save it. However, that depends not only on the Brazilian government, multinational corporations, and multilateral organizations such as the World Bank, but also on consumers in the developed world.

Notes

1. "WWF/World Bank Forest Alliance: Brazil: Facts." http://www-esd. worldbank.org/wwf/ff.htm. Internet. (17 Nov 1999).

2. Silber, Susan and William Velton. "Fact Sheet K2—Tropical Rainforest Animals." *Rainforest Action Network.* http://www.ran.org/ran/info_center/ factsheets/k2.html. Internet. (1 Mar 2001).

3. Silber, Susan and William Velton. "Fact Sheet K2—Tropical Rainforest Animals." *Rainforest Action Network.* http://www.ran.org/ran/info_center/ factsheets/k2.html. Internet. (1 Mar 2001).

4. Rainforest Action Network and PBS Online. "Science in the Rainforest: 66 Rainforest Facts." http://www.pbs.org/tal/costa_rica/facts.html. Internet. (9 Nov 1999).

5. "WWF/World Bank Forest Alliance: Brazil: Facts." http://www-esd. worldbank.org/wwf/ff.htm. Internet. (17 Nov 1999).

6. Greenpeace. "Brazil: Rainforest Under Siege." http://www.greenpeace. org/~comms/cbio/brazil.html. Internet. (22 Feb 2001).

7. "Quinine." Funk & Wagnalls Multimedia Encyclopedia. Funk & Wagnalls. 1999. (11 Nov 1999).

8. "Quinine." Funk & Wagnalls Multimedia Encyclopedia. Funk & Wagnalls. 1999. (11 Nov 1999).

9. Rainforest Action Network. "Factsheet 3B—Species Extinction." http:// www.ran.org/ran/info_center/factsheets/03b.html. Internet. (1 Mar 2001).

10. Calculated from statistics found on "WWF/World Bank Forest Alliance: Brazil: Facts." http://www-esd.worldbank.org/wwf/ff.htm. Internet. (17 Nov 1999).

11. Rainforest Action Network. "Fact Sheet 1D—Facts about the Rainforests." http://www.ran.org/info_center/factsheets/01d.html. Internet. (1 Dec 2000).

12. Mullen, Leslie. "Welcome to Thunder Dome: Atlanta's Urban Heat Alters Weather Patterns." *Science @ NASA.* National Aeronautics and Space Administration. http://science.nasa.gov/newhome/headlines/essd26apr99_1.htm. Internet. (11 Nov 1999).

13. Mullen, Leslie. "Welcome to Thunder Dome: Atlanta's Urban Heat Alters Weather Patterns." *Science @ NASA.* National Aeronautics and Space Administration. http://science.nasa.gov/newhome/headlines/essd26apr99_1.htm. Internet. (11 Nov 1999).

14. Danaher, Mike. "What Price The Environment?: An Analysis of Japanese Public Awareness of Environmental Issues." http://mcel.pacificu.edu/ aspac/scholars/Danaher/danaher.html. Internet. (11 Nov 1999).

15. Danaher, Mike. "What Price The Environment?: An Analysis of Japanese Public Awareness of Environmental Issues." http://mcel.pacificu.edu/ aspac/scholars/Danaher/danaher.html. Internet. (11 Nov 1999).

16. Danaher, Mike. "What Price The Environment?: An Analysis of Japanese Public Awareness of Environmental Issues." http://mcel.pacificu.edu/ aspac/scholars/Danaher/danaher.html. Internet. (11 Nov 1999).

17. World Wildlife Fund. "Mahogany's Survival Threatened by U.S. Demand." *World Wildlife Fund Newsroom.* http://www.worldwildlife.org/news/

headline.cfm?newsid=195. Internet. (2 Mar 2001).

18. Rainforest Action Network and PBS Online. "Science in the Rainforest: Action Alert 114: Loggers Raid Amazon for Mahogany!" http://www.pbs.org/tal/costa_rica/res2/aa114.html. Internet. (7 Nov 1999).

19. Rainforest Action Network and PBS Online. "Science in the Rainforest: Action Alert 114: Loggers Raid Amazon for Mahogany!" http://www.pbs.org/tal/costa_rica/res2/aa114.html. Internet. (7 Nov 1999).

20. Rainforest Action Network and PBS Online. "Science in the Rainforest: Action Alert 114: Loggers Raid Amazon for Mahogany!" http://www.pbs.org/tal/costa_rica/res2/aa114.html. Internet. (7 Nov 1999).

21. Gamini, Gabriella. "Race to Save the Amazon Basin." *The Times* (London). 19 December 2000. Lexis-Nexis Academic Universe. American University Library, Washington, D.C.

22. Smith, Nigel J.H. *Rainforest Corridors: The Transamazon Colonization Scheme.* Berkeley: University of California Press, 1982.

23. Smith, Nigel J.H. *Rainforest Corridors: The Transamazon Colonization Scheme.* Berkeley: University of California Press, 1982.

24. Smith, Nigel J.H. *Rainforest Corridors: The Transamazon Colonization Scheme.* Berkeley: University of California Press, 1982.

25. Smith, Nigel J.H. *Rainforest Corridors: The Transamazon Colonization Scheme.* Berkeley: University of California Press, 1982.

26. Smith, Nigel J.H. *Rainforest Corridors: The Transamazon Colonization Scheme.* Berkeley: University of California Press, 1982.

27. Browder, John and Brian Godfrey. *Rainforest Cities: Urbanization, Development, and Globalization of the Brazilian Amazon.* New York: Columbia University Press, 1997.

28. Smith, Nigel J.H. *Rainforest Corridors: The Transamazon Colonization Scheme.* Berkeley: University of California Press, 1982.

29. Smith, Nigel J.H. *Rainforest Corridors: The Transamazon Colonization Scheme.* Berkeley: University of California Press, 1982.

30. Smith, Nigel J.H. *Rainforest Corridors: The Transamazon Colonization Scheme.* Berkeley: University of California Press, 1982.

31. Smith, Nigel J.H. *Rainforest Corridors: The Transamazon Colonization Scheme.* Berkeley: University of California Press, 1982.

32. Browder, John and Brian Godfrey. *Rainforest Cities: Urbanization, Development, and Globalization of the Brazilian Amazon.* New York: Columbia University Press, 1997.

33. Smith, Nigel J.H. *Rainforest Corridors: The Transamazon Colonization Scheme.* Berkeley: University of California Press, 1982.

34. Browder, John and Brian Godfrey. *Rainforest Cities: Urbanization, Development, and Globalization of the Brazilian Amazon.* New York: Columbia University Press, 1997.

35. World Bank Group. "Sustainable Settlement in the Amazon." Book Abstract. http://www.worldbank.org/html/extpb/abshtml/61104.htm. Internet. (17 Nov 1999).

36. World Wildlife Fund. "WWF-US: World Wildlife Fund—Endangered Species."

http://www.worldwildlife.org/global200/spacessection.cfm?newspaperid=20&sectionid=115&contentid=170. Internet. (1 Mar 2001).

37. United Nations Research Institute for Social Development. "The Social Dynamics of Deforestation in the Amazon: An Overview." http://www.unrisd.org/engindex/publ/list/dp/dp36/dp36-06.htm. Internet. (17 Nov 1999).

38. Browder, John and Brian Godfrey. *Rainforest Cities: Urbanization, Development, and Globalization of the Brazilian Amazon.* New York: Columbia University Press, 1997.

39. Browder, John and Brian Godfrey. *Rainforest Cities: Urbanization, Development, and Globalization of the Brazilian Amazon.* New York: Columbia University Press, 1997.

40. "Brazil—External Debt." Graph. *Latin Focus.* http://www.latin-focus.com/countries/brazil/bradebt.htm. Internet. (2 Mar 2001).

41. "Boycott Mitsubishi." http://bcn.boulder.co.us/environment/earthfirst/Mitsubishi/Mitsu.htm. Internet. (15 Nov 1999).

42. "Brazil—External Debt." Graph. *Latin Focus.* http://www.latin-focus.com/countries/brazil/bradebt.htm. Internet. (3 Mar 2001).

43. Rainforest Action Network and PBS Online. "Science in the Rainforest: 66 Rainforest Facts." http://www.pbs.org/tal/costa_rica/facts.html. Internet. (9 Nov 1999).

44. World Bank Group. "World Bank/WWF Forest Alliance." http://www-esd.worldbank.org/wwf/back2.htm. Internet. (17 Nov 1999).

45. World Bank Group. "WWF/World Bank Forest Alliance: Brazil: Facts." http://www-esd.worldbank.org/wwf/ff.htm. Internet. (17 Nov 1999).

2

The Amazon Rain Forest Is Not in Danger of Being Destroyed

Marc Morano

Marc Morano is a correspondent for American Investigator, *a television newsmagazine, and co-producer with Kent Washburn of* Amazon Rainforest: Clear-Cutting the Myths.

There has been talk for years about the destruction of the Amazon rain forest. However, the Amazon is one of the most intact and least-endangered forests on the planet. The claim that the rain forests are being destroyed "at a rate of 20 football fields a minute" is false. In addition, claims that the Amazon serves as the "lungs of the earth" and that over "450 species" are destroyed every day in the Amazon are exaggerated. The Amazon is not in as much danger as some environmentalists think. More than 87 percent of the forest is still intact. Instead, what is in danger of extinction are the native people of the Amazon rain forest who are prevented by stringent environmental regulations from using the forest to support themselves.

The TV newsmagazine *American Investigator* looked into the claims about the Amazon made by environmental groups and celebrity activists and found that most of the hype is dead wrong. Yet Patrick Moore, a founding and former member of Greenpeace, says that "only 10 percent of the Amazon has been converted to date from what was original forest to agriculture and settlement."

According to Landsat satellite imaging and analysis carried out at the National Institute for Research in Amazonia, the rain forest is much greener than expected. As detailed in the recent TV special, *Amazon Rainforest: Clear-Cutting the Myths*, Landsat data indicate that 87.5 percent of the forest is still intact. Of the 12.5 percent that is deforested, one-third to one-half is in the process of regeneration, meaning that up to 94 percent of the Amazon rain forest is left to nature.

Philip Stott of the University of London and author of the new book, *Tropical Rainforests: Political and Hegemonic Myth-Making*, maintains that the environmental campaigns have lost perspective.

"One of the simple, but very important, facts is that the rain forests have only been around for between 12,000 and 16,000 years," he says. "That sounds like a very long time, but in terms of the history of the Earth, it's hardly a pinprick. The simple point is that there are now still, despite what humans have done, more rain forests today than there were 12,000 years ago."

Moore adds that "the rain forests of the Amazon, the Congo, Malaysia, Indonesia and a few other parts of the world are the least-endangered forests" because "they are the least suitable for human habitation."

Despite the Amazon being at least 87.5 percent intact, many claims abound as to how fast the forest is being cleared.

Fact or fiction: destruction claims

In the widely viewed 1985 TV documentary *Amazonia,* produced by the World Wildlife Fund, the narrator intones that "in the brief amount of time it takes to watch this film, roughly 400,000 acres of forest will have been cleared." Ruy de Goes of Greenpeace-Brazil says that in the last four years "an area the size of France was destroyed."

Actor William Shatner in a *National Geographic* documentary claims that, worldwide, "rain forest is being cleared at a rate of 20 football fields a minute." Rainforest Action Network says the Amazon is being deforested at a rate of eight football fields a minute. Tim Keating of Rainforest Relief says that worldwide deforestation can be measured in seconds. "It may be closer to two to three football fields a second," says Keating.

The simple point is that there are now still, despite what humans have done, more rain forests today than there were 12,000 years ago.

When de Goes of Greenpeace-Brazil is confronted with the disparity in numbers regarding these football fields, he replies, "The numbers are not important; what is important is that there is huge destruction going on." However, Moore says that the only way such huge numbers are generated is by using double accounting. "You would have cleared 50 times the size of the Amazon already if accurate."

Luis Almir, an official with the state of Amazonas in Brazil, calculated using five football fields a minute and sarcastically concludes that, if the numbers were correct, "we would have a desert bigger than the Sahara."

Lungs of the Earth

Another familiar claim of the environmentalist community is that the Amazon constitutes the "lungs of the Earth," supplying one-fifth of the world's oxygen. But, according to the Institute for Research in Amazonia and other eco-scientists, the Amazon consumes as much oxygen as it produces, and Stott says it actually may be a net user of oxygen.

"In fact, because the trees fall down and decay, rain forests actually take in slightly more oxygen than they give out," says Stott. "The idea of them soaking up carbon dioxide and giving out oxygen is a myth. It's only fast-growing young trees that actually take up carbon dioxide."

Biodiversity loss

Many environmentalists claim that as many as 50,000 species are being driven to extinction every year because of the destruction of tropical forests such as the Amazon. Rainforest Relief's Keating weighs in with a hefty "450 species lost per day." These estimates are rooted in the research of Harvard University [professor] Edward O. Wilson, who based it on computer models of the potential, but as yet undiscovered, species that may be going extinct yearly.

The Amazon consumes as much oxygen as it produces, and . . . it actually may be a net user of oxygen.

"There is no scientific basis for saying that 50,000 species are going extinct," says Greenpeace cofounder Moore. "I want a list of Latin species." Moore maintains no one can name these species that are said to be going extinct. "The only place you can find them is in Edward O. Wilson's computer at Harvard University. They're actually electrons on a hard drive," Moore states.

When asked if he can name a single species of the 50,000 that are said to be going extinct, Keating admits: "No we cannot, because we don't know what those species are."

Moore is flabbergasted by such statements. "You're telling me that I'm supposed to prove that those species didn't go extinct when they're not there anymore and we never knew they were there in the first place?" Moore asks. "That's impossible. I don't know how Wilson can truck out the number 50,000 and keep a straight face."

Fear of fire

Another claim the environmental movement makes is that fires are destroying the Amazon. In recent years, it was reported that fires in the late 1990s equaled or even surpassed those of the peak "burning season" of the eighties. The Woods Hole Research Institute maintains that as much as half of the Amazon rain forest is "a tinderbox about to go up in flames."

Moore counters: "To say that half of the Amazon rain forest is going to go up in smoke is just crazy. Of course it's not. That's completely ridiculous and extremist. But, let's say a large portion of the rain forest burned. The next thing that will happen is it will grow back again."

Stott believes the more scrutiny the "Save-the-Amazon" cause gets, the more the bad science will be exposed.

"When we actually look at these myths—this is what is terrifying about them—when we look at the science, we suddenly find that these myths are just insupportable—or 'unsustainable,' to use a nice green term. They just don't make sense."

Keating, who calls the destruction of rain forests "the greatest ecological catastrophe," nonetheless concedes that the Amazon "is still the largest area of tropical rain forest left on Earth and has probably the lowest volume of clearing that has occurred of any large rain-forest areas in the world."

Moore, however, believes that, despite all evidence to the contrary, the conventional wisdom that the Amazon is about to disappear will remain the conventional wisdom for some time. He says, "If people . . . actually go to the Amazon, go to Manaus, get on a river boat and go up or down the Amazon for hundreds of miles, go inland and look for yourself or fly over it, [they] will see that you can fly for three hours over solid forest and really not see any sign of human habitation. It is not all burning up. It has not all been destroyed. And there really is no chance that it will be in the foreseeable future."

The real danger

The real cost of the Save-the-Amazon movement has been paid by the poverty-stricken residents of Brazil. Brazilians complain that the international environmental and celebrity campaigns to save the Amazon have harmed Brazil's ability to develop infrastructure and help the millions in poverty there. But just how do the environmentalists define poverty?

Keating believes that there are a lot of "misperceptions about poverty." He says, "We perceive people to be poor if they don't have running water, they don't have electricity. I mean we humans have existed without electricity and running water for many, many thousands of years and, geez, we weren't extinct as a species."

To say that half of the Amazon rain forest is going to go up in smoke is just crazy. Of course it's not.

The poor who inhabit the river banks of the Amazon have felt the increasingly stringent environmental regulations supported by Keating. "The police have forbidden me," says Caboclo villager Janio Oliveira, "not to do anything that would harm the forest, like cutting trees. If they catch me, I will have to pay a fine and possibly go to prison." Fabio Ferreira notes that environmentalists have come to his village and have "exaggerated the point to tell us that we don't even have a right to walk through the jungle because it will destroy the ecosystem on that path." Oliveira's grandmother, Deuzita, asks, "If people don't let us use the forest, what will we survive off of? And if people stop us we'll die eventually."

Celebrity crusades

Despite the prevailing poverty in Brazil, celebrity activists lobby to keep out economic development and growth in Brazil. Actor Chevy Chase goes so far as to say capitalism is not the answer for the poor, maintaining that "sometimes socialism works" to help people out of poverty. He adds, "I think it's conclusive that there have been areas where socialism has helped to keep people at least stabilized at a certain level." Chase believes that "Cuba might prove that." Actor Tom Arnold makes no bones about controlling development in the poorer nations. "It is arrogant, but we are going to have to help them. It's what's going to have to happen," he opines.

If people don't let us use the forest, what will we survive off of? And if people stop us we'll die eventually.

Jayni Chase, wife of Chevy and head of the environmental group Friends of the Earth, justifies the poverty in Brazil because "environmentalists are trying to think long term, not just feed your child tomorrow. We're trying to think long term." Robert Whelan, the author of *The Myth of the Noble Eco-Savage*, counters, "It's very easy to romanticize these things from a distance, as long as it's not your children who are dying without medical care."

Laurie Parise, the executive director of musician Sting's Rainforest Foundation, doesn't dispute that the Amazon is nearly 90 percent intact. She counters instead that the intentions matter, "I know in my heart that we're doing the right thing."

Rio de Janeiro engineer Guillerme Camargo opines that "we feel, as Brazilians, that living standards are being denied to us under such false arguments, under such false excuses. Why can't we have the same living standards like Europeans, like Americans?"

Sorry Brazil, environmentalists and celebrities are more in tune with the feel-good cause than with the facts.

3

Canada's Rain Forest Is in Danger

B.J. Bergman

B.J. Bergman is a writer and editor for Sierra, *a magazine that promotes conservation of natural resources.*

The Great Bear rain forest, an 8-million-acre expanse along the north-central coast of British Columbia, is the largest intact temperate rain forest in the world. This Canadian rain forest is the only place in the world to find the white Kermode bear, or spirit bear. It is estimated that 230 bird species and 68 different mammals reside there as well. However, like other rain forests, the Great Bear rain forest has been threatened by excessive logging and destruction. The logging industry threatens not only the wildlife, but also the Heiltsuk, an Indian tribe that lives there.

It's a logy Saturday morning—too early for more than a strong dose of airport coffee—but it doesn't take a topo map to discern some faultlines in Canada's famously placid national psyche. The English, it seems, find Canadians a bloody bore, and the *Globe and Mail*'s "In London" columnist is in a snit, albeit a mild one. Rallying to the defense of her homeland, she whips out her trump card, the incontrovertible proof of *interestingness*: "We are, after all, a country that has tamed the wilderness."

I'm mulling this curious boast when my plane starts its descent into Port Hardy, near the northern tip of Vancouver Island. On cue, the landscape comes into focus as a chain of clearcuts, gash upon gash of stumps that look like scars on the piney green flesh of the earth. Entering British Columbia the night before, Elyssa Rosen, a Sierra Club staffer from California, gingerly told the customs agent she was part of "a conservation group" planning to tour "the Great Bear Rainforest." The officer's posture of studied, half-hearted welcome fell away. "You're not *protesting*, are you?" she demanded. "Because we don't like that here."

Her fears, while not unfounded, were misplaced. The forest we are headed for is reachable only by boat or floatplane, far too remote for mass demonstrations. "Great Bear Rainforest" is the name conservationists

Reprinted from B.J. Bergman, "Canada's Forgotten Coast," *Sierra*, March/April 1999. Permission conveyed through Copyright Clearance Center, Inc.

have conferred upon an 8-million-acre expanse along 300 miles of British Columbia's north-central coast, the largest intact temperate rainforest left on the globe. "Intact," of course, is a relative term: many of the hundreds of watersheds here, like those to the south, have been chewed up by chainsaws, and timber companies have sewn up the logging rights to virtually the entire ecosystem. Yet the Great Bear has a still-beating heart of some 50 virgin watersheds, most of them larger than 10,000 acres, and so sustains a wealth of wildlife, including one creature found nowhere else in the world: the white Kermode, or spirit bear, actually a black bear with a double-recessive gene that gives it a coat the color of vanilla custard. An estimated 230 bird species live here, bald eagles among them, as do 68 different mammals, including grizzlies and wolves, and all have coexisted for millennia with nine First Nations, the Canadian counterparts of Native American tribes. But these residents are no match for timber executives intent on quarterly earnings, or government ministers for whom thousand-year-old cedars and 300-foot spruce are grandest on their way to the mill. The Great Bear Rainforest could soon become the next Vancouver Island, where only a handful of major watersheds remain unlogged. And that's precisely why we're here.

But we haven't come to protest, just to explore. And then, when we've had an eyeful, to make some noise back in the States, which consumes the bulk of British Columbia's old-growth timber and ought to know better. Compared to a forest, it turns out, a tamed wilderness isn't all that interesting.

Many of the hundreds of watersheds here . . . have been chewed up by chainsaws, and timber companies have sewn up the logging rights to virtually the entire ecosystem.

The coastal village of Bella Bella is nearly desolate when we arrive; there's a funeral in progress, though we won't know whose for several days. Merran Smith, the B.C. Sierra Club's energetic forest organizer, and a few young accomplices shuttle our gear to the *Sundown*, a strikingly handsome 62-foot yacht that first saw service in 1924 as a floating hardware store. The ship's current owner and captain, Joseph Bettis, is equally striking, if not quite so handsome, a white-bearded, bib-overalled, Zen-spouting salt with a twang straight out of west Texas. After lunch he gives us the house rules and the nickel tour, then repairs to the wheelhouse and we're off. Everywhere the tree-lined hills rise and disappear into a preternatural mist.

I get my first real taste of rainforest after dinner. A half-dozen of us borrow a small motorcraft from the top deck of the *Sundown*, then traipse through a soggy patch of dense, fragrant forest until we reach Kisameet Lake. Merran, a Vancouverite with a perverse fondness for cold water, talks us into a swim. It's nearly dark and we wade in cautiously until there's no choice but total submersion. The water is frigid—even in late July—and I'm soon perched on a rock again, rubbing myself for warmth, bathed in mist and silence and the sweet smell of cedar. A bald eagle glides overhead, commanding and unmistakable in the lingering twilight.

In Indian culture, somebody says, eagles are messengers of the Creator. We are quiet a long time after that, trying to make out the message.

A handwritten sign taped to the door of the market says the proprietors will be back soon, a cheap irony. Namu is a ghost town. Only it's not a town so much as a glorified encampment, a turn-of-the-century cannery complex floating at the edge of the forest like a great barge. The place was still humming 30 years ago. Now the market is padlocked, but everything else seems to have been hurriedly abandoned, from ramshackle cottages to a gym with a beat-up parquet floor. Several of us take turns posing for snapshots at the decaying counter of the unlocked cafe, whose sign reads "Open."

To the timber industry, a forest is a crop to be harvested when it's ripe and then replanted, like cabbage.

Cannery workers are an indicator species. Namu is what happens when waterways teem with fish, and then they don't.

We walk for a while, sticking close to Bristol Foster, a British Columbian biologist who points out the local flora—salal, skunk cabbage, sphagnum moss—and encourages us to sample the elderberries, thimbleberries, and juicy, heart-shaped salmonberries. He shows us the difference between Western red cedar and the more fragrant, droopier yellow cedar, which, until the bottom fell out of the market, commanded especially high prices in Japan. We find otter and wolf tracks, recent but not fresh. We visit a midden where an archaeological dig turned up evidence of 10,000 years of human habitation.

It's in Namu that we hook up with Merran's partner, filmmaker Mike Simpson, who ferries us in his motorized rubber Zodiac to the shallow mouth of the nearby Koeye River. This is serious bear country, a stunningly green estuary that seems, as we begin to hike, less forest than pasture, an enormous sedge meadow flecked with Indian paintbrush and ringed by tall trees and gun-metal hills. Then the meadow recedes, and soon we're half-bushwhacking along a whispery bear trail through dense underbrush and prickly devil's club, past "mark trees" on which bears, for reasons of their own, have scratched their graffiti and rubbed their fur into the bark, and "culturally modified trees," old-growth red cedars whose trunks were once chiseled by Native people for canoes or longhouses and then left to heal. Amid the huge cedar and Sitka spruce are hemlocks and other small trees that have taken root in fallen nurse logs, testimony to the cyclical nature of things. Bristol identifies the whistle of the varied thrush, "the sound of the rainforest," and briefly flushes one out of hiding with distressed-bird calls. Moss covers everything from the canopy to the forest floor, and it is all dark and wet and wonderful, the living archetype of dreams and fairy tales.

Bristol stoops to sift a soggy handful of earth. Temperate rainforests, he tells us, are even richer in biomass than tropical ones, and can have as many as 10,000 species of bacteria in a cubic centimeter of soil. This statistic sings to me like a haiku. It gives shape to my sense of infinite vitality, of having entered a world beyond our capacity to fathom or control. We mess with it at our peril.

Yet it is being messed with. Worse, it is being cold-bloodedly hacked to pieces. British Columbia timber companies are clearcutting in valley bottoms and along fish-bearing streams, tearing up rainforest for roads into previously untouched watersheds. To the timber industry, a forest is a crop to be harvested when it's ripe and then replanted, like cabbage. Industry jargon for these ancient trees is "decadent." What's the use of a thousand-year-old tree?

We were traumatized as a people. The miracle is that we have survived.

Merran finds a salmon jaw, dropped by an eagle, possibly, or left behind by a griz. We hike until we reach some ancient bear tracks, and we follow (as have the bear themselves, for hundreds or thousands of years) in the creatures' prodigious footsteps. We fail to spot any bear, even after five hours on their trail. But it's only our first full day in the rainforest.

The Heiltsuk

Back in Bella Bella, Merran and I find ourselves at the home of Don Vickers, an affable, soft-spoken man who used to work at the Namu cannery. This village is inhabited mainly by members of the Heiltsuk band, a First Nation that once lived fat off salmon-rich streams hereabouts and knows this spit as Waglisla. Vickers, a Heiltsuk hereditary chief, owns a small cabin in the Ingram-Mooto Lakes region to the north, where Western Forest Products is busy cutting a logging road. He describes how, a few months earlier, some 75 Heiltsuk—drummers, dancers, and chiefs in full regalia—staged a protest in the Ingram. The company agreed to suspend the operation, but was back blasting within weeks. "They've never had any respect before," Vickers says. "I guess they won't show any now."

The Heiltsuk, Vickers explains, have always depended on fish, and fish top the list of collateral damage in the buzz-saw barrage on the rainforest. Salmon stocks have plummeted as logging dumps silt into streams and roadbuilding wreaks havoc on spawning grounds, exacerbating the impacts of decades of commercial overfishing. Vickers says that with the band's survival at stake, many Heiltsuk would be open to logging, if only it meant jobs for their people. But it rarely does, and Vickers is increasingly unsure what the future holds. "What's going to be left for our grandchildren, the way things are going?" he wonders. "It makes me sick sometimes to think what they've taken out."

He is not alone. A group of ten hereditary chiefs has agreed to meet with us, which is something of an event; First Nations tend to regard environmentalists with suspicion. Our two groups, Natives and outlanders, muster at the church. Following introductions, Pauline Waterfall—the daughter of a chief who acquired her mellifluous surname by marrying an Englishman—leads us in a prayer. "O Great Spirit," it begins. "We thank you for the abundance you have given us. . . ."

But abundance, history shows, is not forever, especially if you're Indian. The Heiltsuk story is depressingly familiar: generations of children hijacked to "residential schools," tribal traditions outlawed, land stolen, resources destroyed. "We were traumatized as a people," Waterfall says in her calm, confident voice. "The miracle is that we have survived."

Under siege from logging operations, the Heiltsuk are by no means of one mind about how to respond; indeed, the crisis has created tensions within the community. The elected tribal council, for example, has been sympathetic to the timber companies, while the hereditary council, the Hemas, has been resistant. But even the hereditary leaders stress that they are not flatly opposed to logging. What they want is a one-year moratorium on roadbuilding and clearcutting. "When people want to come here to harvest our resources we need to have something to say about it," asserts Harvey Humchitt, a traditional chief and the spokesman for the Hemas council. "We've been here a long time."

After two hours, Waterfall brings the meeting to a close. "The Creator always provides opportunities for growth amid chaos," she observes, adding: "You're a human being first. When you look at it that way, it gives us a way to work together." As if to prove her point, waiting for us at the dock is Larry Jorgenson, a cigar-chewing social worker who married into the Heiltsuk a quarter-century ago. His adopted people, he insists, are "an integral part of the ecosystem." The Heiltsuk's future, like their past, is one with the rainforest.

Despite the pleas of the Heiltsuk, despite the slump in timber prices, Western Forest Products is plunging ahead with a major logging road here in the Great Bear's core.

Over the next 24 hours, Jorgenson shows us just what he means. He takes us first to a Heiltsuk winter residence abandoned perhaps 150 years ago; a husky Sitka spruce has taken root around a cedar beam that formed the foundation of the longhouse. Then we motor through The Gate up to Deer Pass, where Jorgenson is overseeing construction of a family-style cabin, part of a project to provide job skills to Heiltsuk youth and restore ancient connections within the community at large. "The sad thing in the last twenty years is the loss of fish, and the loss of ties to the land," he says. With smaller salmon streams drying up, Native people are forced to resort to deeper, more dangerous spots like Purple Bluff, where, he reports—solving the mystery of that funeral in Bella Bella—two Heiltsuk drowned just a few days earlier fishing for sockeye. "They never used to fish there," Jorgenson says.

Next day we visit the base of an ancient Heiltsuk burial cairn, which Jorgenson found only a month before. It is near a series of pictographs, which Jorgenson believes indicate burial sites throughout the rainforest. How much more of the Heiltsuk's cultural history is yet undiscovered? Nobody knows. And that, Jorgenson says, is why it's imperative that we "stop the logging insanity."

Logging continues

As we snake our way up the coast, the hillside clearcuts visible from the *Sundown* are relatively small, a few acres usually, and alder is coming in where cedar used to be. The Ingram valley is more disturbing. Despite the pleas of the Heiltsuk, despite the slump in timber prices, Western Forest Products is plunging ahead with a major logging road here in the Great Bear's core, one of 40 key ecological areas identified by forest activists. In May 1998, stepped-up public opposition to logging forced International Forest Products, or Interfor, to abort a road it was gouging into the Johnston watershed, south of the Koeye River. In Europe, an important market for B.C. timber, retailers have been hammered by a high-profile consumer campaign led by Greenpeace, and now the noose is tightening closer to home. Western apparently figures the percentage play is to get in while it can.

For the moment at least, Canada has not tamed its wilderness.

Western's security squad is busy when we arrive unannounced at the logging camp. But not on our account. A British television reporter is being choppered in, a prime opportunity for the timber giant to export a favorite domestic theme: the industry regrets its past mistakes, and is now logging responsibly and sustainably. The foreman warily grants us permission to look around.

The six of us head out along a dirt road the width of a two-lane highway. It's an uphill hike, and in just a few minutes I'm aware of an odd sensation: it's hot. There's no canopy, no shade. We trudge past idled earth-movers and leveled trees lined up like guardrails alongside the road. After a while we spot a cluster of humans, some in bright-orange hard hats. Among them is Zoe Stephenson, who's conducting research for a BBC program on Canadian logging. We insinuate ourselves into the cluster, and before long Merran has thoroughly upstaged the company tour guides, explaining to the attentive researcher why the industry's trumpeted forestry reforms are a hoax and describing how current practices imperil the rainforest. This is pure theater, really; Stephenson is scheduled to meet with Sierra Club staff in Vancouver in a day or two. But the company reps don't know this, and they stand around helplessly, glancing at their watches, until we move on up the road.

The Ingram valley is surpassingly lovely, all the more because it is vanishing under our noses. As we approach the crystalline lake we hear a blast of explosives, the first in a series, and we know the BBC has left the site.

With just three days to reach the town of Prince Rupert, near the Alaska border, Captain Joseph picks up the pace; the coast takes on a dreamlike quality, an ethereal image of green glacial water moving through unending forested mountainsides. The dream, however, is punctuated by happy accidents. One afternoon a group of us hop in the Zodiac for a quick impromptu trip to the mouth of Kynoch Inlet and wind up navigating its entire length, pulled along by spectacular, Yosemite-like views of sheer granite cliffs and stark, glorious solitude. Later, while the rest of the group takes in the scenery from the deck of the *Sundown*, several of us motor to Roderick Island, expecting to find an active logging camp. When we arrive, though, it resembles Namu, abandoned but for a lone caretaker. He allows that the operation was shut down a week earlier, a casualty of the depressed timber market.

After several days of flukishly clear skies, the customary overcast returns on Thursday. Most of us are just having our breakfast as we cruise past Princess Royal Island, principal habitat of the spirit bear. We're peering hopefully out the galley windows when somebody calls us to the forward deck, where eight Dall's porpoises are playfully escorting the *Sundown* northward, hamming it up with synchronized rolls under the bow. A bit later we spot a pod of orcas about 50 yards from the ship. We watch as the killer whales herd salmon in the shallow water, the fish tracing silver arcs as they try to make their getaways.

Then the whales, too, disappear, and Mike takes us in shifts to the mouth of the waterfall-fed Khutze River, where we set off on foot along the estuary. We find bald eagles perched on overhanging branches, marbled murrelets diving under the water. There are bear and wolf tracks, and divots where bear have pulled up rice roots and angelica, and a cozy lair in a cedar stump. But we don't see any bear, spirit or otherwise.

The Spirit Bear

It's not till our last full day that we glimpse the true spirit of the Great Bear Rainforest. Only it's not bear, I realize. It's salmon. Near Lowe Inlet we note a profusion of sockeye, and we trail them to what looks like a Class IV rapid, the kind that gives fits to rafters going downriver. The salmon are swimming upstream, into the whitewater wall. I sit on a rock beside the cataract for an hour, watching as one fish after another vaults determinedly into the foam, usually to be knocked fin over teakettle and deposited back at the bottom. It's an amazing display of unalloyed will, and each time a fish clears the hurdle it's cause for rejoicing, one small but crucial victory in the survival Olympics. Significant levels of the "salmon signature," the N15 nitrogen isotope, have been found in the cellulose of trees, indicating that when bears drag salmon into the forest the remains feed not only other wild creatures but the cedar and spruce themselves; Ian McAllister, a founder of the Raincoast Conservation Society, likes to say that the trees here are really "salmon trees," the bear "salmon bear." Everything, in a way, depends on salmon. And it's going the way of the buffalo.

But the *Globe and Mail* columnist got it wrong. For the moment, at least, Canada has not tamed its wilderness. The Great Bear Rainforest survives, and with it the Heiltsuk people, the spirit bear, the grizzly, the wolf, the bald eagle, a remnant of time that seemed to have been lost forever. And maybe that, after all, was the eagle's message in the twilight at Kisameet Lake: the Creator is here, still. For the moment.

Indigenous Tribes of the Rain Forest Are in Danger

Sebastião Salgado

*Sebastião Salgado is considered one of the world's greatest photojour-
nalists. In 1994, he embarked on a six-year project for* Rolling Stone
*magazine, documenting mass displacement of people by war, economic
change, and environmental ruin at the end of the twentieth century.*

As the rain forest continues to be the target of destruction, not
only are trees and animal species threatened, but so are the rain
forest's indigenous tribes. The Yanonmami, Macuxi, and Marubo
are three Brazilian Indian tribes whose cultures have been threatened to the point of extinction by an invasion of cattle ranchers,
gold and diamond miners, and timber merchants. With the invasion of modernism and industry these Indian tribes are losing
many of their traditions and customs; many have abandoned the
traditional ways of dress, opting instead for jeans and T-shirts,
while others no longer hunt and fish for food but now buy their
food and supplies from the local military base. This invasion has
also brought prostitution, weapon bartering, and foreign diseases
to this once pristine and secluded rain forest. Proposals to set aside
preserved territories for the indigenous tribes have been met with
opposition by powerful Brazilian business groups—primarily cattle ranchers and timber companies. The future is bleak for the rain
forest and its indigenous tribes as both continue to be the target
of destruction.

One of the most potent symbols for the native tribes in the Amazon
River valley, the most threatening omen that their way of life will
soon disappear, is the road. Because once a road is set into the forest, once
the lanes are surveyed, the trees cleared, the soil leveled and paved over,
then come the trucks, the noise, the trash, the disease and, in the end,
still-wider roads. And before the steam settles over the first freshly paved
roads, the cultures of the indigenous people are forever altered. In the fall
of 1998, I spent forty days traveling through two distinct areas of the
Brazilian frontier: the northern state of Roraima, which abuts Venezuela

and Guyana, home to the Yanomami; and, farther south, the Javarí valley, which runs along the Solimões River (known outside Brazil as the upper Amazon).

Brazilian Indian tribes

[The cultures of] three Indian tribes: the Yanomami, Macuxi and Marubo, have been pushed to the brink of extinction by the invasion of cattle ranchers, gold and diamond miners and timber merchants. They have suffered to such an extent that one of the Macuxi tribe leaders has declared, "The white man has built roads, houses, farms and opened the way to disease, poverty and death." The most precious elements that have been lost, the ones that can never be reintroduced to the habitat, are the traditions of the tribes. Indian mores that have endured for hundreds of years have now been rubbed from the surface of Amazonia.

I first visited and photographed the tribal territories in the Amazon in the mid-Eighties, while working with a group of Brazilian scientists studying a rare African illness known as river blindness, which had inexplicably appeared in Brazil. We camped in the Yanomami territory and were warmed by the openness and hospitality of the Indians. They happily guided us through the thickets and fed and sheltered us without complaint. On this trip to the rain forest, I witnessed a devastation so complete, so sweeping, that it seemed a century had elapsed since my last visit. It's as though a chain reaction is taking place, each stage stripping away yet another layer of history and stability from the tribes.

This chain begins with the Brazilian military. During my first visit, I came across a simple airstrip in the jungle near the Yanomami village Surucucu that had been built for very small planes, planes that could carry two to four people. Today there's a massive military airport staffed by perhaps thousands of soldiers, who are patrolling the border with Venezuela.

The white man has built roads, houses, farms and opened the way to disease, poverty and death.

In September 1998, I flew by helicopter into this airport. I was shocked as a chief in the Yanomami tribe greeted me on the tarmac clothed in camouflage pants and vest. Thirteen years ago, I could hardly have conceived of a tribal chief wearing clothes, much less military surplus.

As the chief escorted me through the village around the base, I saw tribesmen decked out in denim and camouflage, some carrying rifles. Traditionally, these men would have lived in expertly crafted wood and grass huts. Now they live in huts cobbled together with plastic and metal scraps gathered from the junk piles around the air base. I saw Yanomami prostitutes openly soliciting soldiers, often as their husbands looked on.

Even the tribal traditions of war, the chief explained to me, have been westernized. At some point in the late Eighties, tribesmen started bartering with the *garimperos*, or miners, beginning the practice of trading sex for rifles. Now, intertribal battles that were once fought with bows and arrows can be waged with these bartered weapons.

The Yanomami are a nomadic tribe, living in one place for a maximum of three years. When the land becomes enfeebled and the stocks of fish become depleted or the game that they hunt become thinned out, the Yanomami move. And they keep moving, gathering their families and dismantling their shacks, loading hunting implements and canoes onto pack mules and setting off for a new jungle to live in, leaving their previous dwelling places to lie fallow. One hundred years might pass before the Yanomami return to a location. They know instinctively, with an accumulated knowledge that is centuries old, that the land can't sustain itself without 100 years' rest. The trees are delicate, the undergrowth is delicate. The soil is poor, and the jungle is not very strong.

Even . . . protected territories are still threatened. The forest is being destroyed, the rivers are polluted . . . [and] vast tracts of wooded land have been ruined.

But all of that has changed. Most Yanomami, especially the ones near the air base, are no longer nomadic. The military has forced them into a state of dependence. Now tribesmen receive food and supplies from the soldiers and have adapted to modern medicine. You see very few Indians hunting or fishing or working the land anymore. You see Yanomami women pregnant by the soldiers; you see flu and rubella epidemics and a population ravaged by venereal diseases imported by the white people. The change is complete, and its speed is awesome.

Demarcation's failures

In 1988, the Brazilian government devised a system to help preserve the territories of the indigenous tribes. The plan, known as demarcation, granted the tribes the legal right to occupy their traditional lands. The tribes can retain autonomy, although the land remains the property of the government. This system, however, hardly solved the problem. Each specific case of demarcation is subject to ratification by the Ministry of Justice, and it becomes official only after the president has approved.

Inevitably, this process has met with the opposition of powerful Brazilian business groups—primarily cattle ranchers and timber and mining companies—which have the tacit support of politicians. The military has also repeatedly stood against demarcation, claiming that ceding control to the Indians would create a security problem. The land that the Yanomami consider their territory lies inside a broad ribbon called the Calha Norte, which the military has set aside as a security buffer. The Calha Norte extends along the borders with Colombia, Venezuela, Guyana, Suriname and French Guiana.

A constitutional amendment in 1988 set a five-year deadline for the final demarcation of all indigenous areas in Brazil. When the deadline passed, on October 5th, 1993, only half of the indigenous lands had been secured by the tribes. And even these protected territories are still threatened. The forest is being destroyed, the rivers are polluted by mining operations, vast tracts of wooded land have been ruined by the damming of the Amazon's tributaries; the roads that are built to haul timber and produce from the river basin exact the most perverse toll on indigenous territories, cutting a swath through the heart of Indian country.

Urban illnesses

Before the 1970s, the Yanomami Indians were an insulated, self-contained community. Except for occasional border skirmishes with rubber-latex extractors, piassava and nut gatherers and hunters, the Yanomami existed peacefully. But in 1973, the Brazilian government began construction on the Perímetro Norte highway, which would eventually extend 200 kilometers through the southern end of the Yanomami territory. The hundreds of nonindigenous workers who built the roads introduced a deadly mix of urban illnesses that infected practically all of the Yanomami villages in one of the region's valleys. Measles and influenza epidemics virtually decimated the tribe. Four of the villages in this area lost twenty-two percent of their population between 1973 and 1975, and four others, in the higher Catrimani valley, lost half of their people in a measles epidemic in 1978.

By 1989, some 50,000 miners had set up operations across the central region of the Yanomami territory in Brazil and crossing the frontier into Venezuela. Mercury and oil polluted the rivers. The coming and going of planes and helicopters frightened the wild game away and left the Yanomami dependent on the miners for food. It is impossible to know how many Indians were killed in armed conflicts with the miners or by contagious diseases brought by the invaders.

Even those communities not directly affected by the presence of miners and their equipment have been hit by the ripple-wave effect of this social, ecological and economic trauma. The conditions among the tribes today read like symptoms on the chart of a dying patient. Mortality rates have skyrocketed; malaria, malnutrition, acute respiratory infections, tuberculosis and worm infections have riven the populations, and even the healthy are infected by such a deep sense of apathy that birth and fertility rates have plunged. The Yanomami villagers today look like a hybrid of the primitive world and the modern world. The changes are evident even in the small details of daily life. Young girls wear banana-leaf brassieres with bluejeans. The hammocks that the Yanomami sleep in, traditionally made from fibers collected in the forest, are now bought in military-surplus stores. The men used to tuck their penises against their bodies. Now they wear shorts.

The Macuxi

The Macuxi, unlike the Yanomami, are not nomadic. Their villages are spread across a once-diverse terrain of hills, savanna and tropical forests, to the north of the Yanomami territory. But the mere fact that the Macuxi were firmly entrenched in the region didn't make them any more immune to the effects of industrial invasion. Their land has proved a rich source of diamonds and gold, and the gentle slopes of the savanna are ideal for raising cattle. The rain forest has been leveled, and the violent erosion that followed choked out the oxygen in the streams and rivers, decimating the fishing stock.

The Macuxi have in the past decade become very passionate about soccer. Some villages even have a television, set up in the village center for the big games. Sporadic access to electricity sets the Macuxi apart from the other tribes in the Amazon. But it means nothing in the face of a monolithic concentration of opponents—the cattle and mining industries, the military and the Brazilian Ministry of Justice, which in 1994 refused to allow demarcation here. But in spite of the relentless series of attacks by the military police, who carry on a battle with the Macuxi dating back more than a century, in 1998 President Fernando Henrique Cardoso announced his intention to honor the original call for demarcation. Now, for a time at least, it's the ranchers and miners who are at odds with the government. The villages are today oddly quiet.

The Marubo

The Indians of the Javarí valley, on the upper stretches of the Amazon River, haven't had as much success. Split into several different tribes, the largest of which is called the Marubo, these peoples are among the most isolated of the tribes of Brazil. The majority of them, like the Yanomami, were once nomadic. But over a period of decades, they settled into malocas, tribal villages erected outside larger towns. The same litany of violence, prejudice and poor living conditions afflicts the Marubo as it does the Yanomami and, to a lesser degree, the Macuxi.

The future of the tribes is bleak. The forces of industry and politics have targeted the Amazon River valley as a nearly limitless source of wealth and resources. The protections that have been legislated in Brasília, the nation's capital, mean very little after three days' walk into the impenetrable jungle. Eventually, camouflage apparel will be commonplace after a week's trek, and soccer games and television and prostitution will be common along the roads of the Amazon.

Rain Forest Wildlife
Is in Danger

John G. Robinson, Kent H. Redford, and Elizabeth L. Bennett

John G. Robinson is vice president of international conservation at the Wildlife Conservation Society (WCS), an organization dedicated to saving wildlife and wild lands throughout the world. Kent H. Redford is director for biodiversity analysis at WCS. Elizabeth L. Bennett is involved in WCS projects in Malaysia.

Commercial logging poses a threat to rain forest wildlife. Commercial logging increases the harvest of wildlife in the rain forest by opening up remote forest areas to increased hunting and consumption of wild meat. The harvest in the Brazilian Amazon is estimated at 9.6 to 23.5 million mammals, birds, and reptiles. Logging also sets off a chain of events in local communities that further increases the threats to wildlife populations. Preventing the excess loss of wildlife is critical to preventing extinction of animal species as well as preventing harm to forest-dwelling people who must live off of the rain forest and its resources.

The international community has responded to the steady loss of tropical rainforests[1] by adopting policies that, rather than strictly protecting these forests, promote their sustainable use.[2] Although there are deep concerns about this approach,[3, 4] there remains a broad consensus that tropical forestry, if modified through policy and technical adjustments, can serve as a conservation strategy by discouraging the conversion of forest lands.[5] However, the increased access to the world's tropical forests has generated a very significant harvest of another resource: wildlife.

Wild meat

This loss of tropical forest wildlife has a direct impact on forest-dwelling people. Ever since they first inhabited rainforests some 40,000 years ago, people have hunted animals for food, and even today most tropical forests are hunted by local peoples.[6-8] The largely subsistence harvest in the Brazilian Amazon is estimated at 67,00 to 164,000 metric tons of wild meat per year.[9] Many tropical forest peoples rely on wild meat for over 50% of their protein.[6, 7, 10] Loss of wildlife resources threatens people's health and well-being and affects their cultural integrity.[11, 12]

The wildlife harvest, even when primarily for subsistence, affects the survival of forest-dwelling animals as well. The harvest in the Brazilian Amazon is estimated at 9.6 to 23.5 million mammals, birds, and reptiles.[9] Almost all species with body masses greater than 1 kg, and sometimes even smaller, are harvested.[6, 7, 9] Even light hunting in the absence of habitat disturbance can significantly depress wildlife populations, and heavy hunting can drive them to local extinction.[7, 13] Many large-bodied, slow-breeding species of special conservation concern [such as great apes, large carnivores, and elephants[14]] are especially vulnerable.

The increased access to the world's tropical forests has generated a very significant harvest of another resource: wildlife.

Finally, the loss of wildlife also threatens the sustainability of tropical forestry itself, because many of the species most affected by hunting are those that play keystone roles in maintaining tropical forests.[13, 15] Most timber-harvesting systems have no provision for regeneration other than natural processes which, in turn, depend on wildlife for tree pollination and seed dispersal. Especially in the neotropics, the seeds of many commercially exploited timber trees are dispersed by large-bodied mammal, bird, and reptile species.[16] Recruitment of timber species depends on maintaining the integrity of these wildlife communities.

Logging affects wildlife harvest

Commercial logging hugely increases the harvest of wildlife from tropical forests by opening up remote forest areas, bringing in people from other regions, and changing local economies and patterns of resource consumption. Every year, logging opens up an additional 50,000 to 59,000 km^2.[17, 18] Logging operations create an extensive network of roads, which link to the national road system. These roads and the trucks that travel them become conduits for a vast commercial trade in wild meat. Meat is transported from remote, previously inaccessible forests for sale in towns. In the tropical forests of Africa, the annual harvest of bushmeat might exceed 1 million metric tons per year, much of it coming through such increased access to forests that are being logged.[19] In kilograms per square kilometer, this harvest is 20 to 50 times greater than the largely subsistence harvest of the Brazilian Amazon. In the Malaysian state of Sarawak in 1996, the wild meat trade was conservatively estimated to be more than 1000 tons per year, with almost all of the meat coming out over logging roads.[20]

Commercial logging also results in the immigration of large numbers of workers into the forest, where they often hunt for their own consumption. Such people are frequently outsiders, living in the area only temporarily, with no incentive to conserve the resource for the future. In Sarawak, for example, the annual catch by hunters in a single logging camp of about 500 people was calculated 1149 animals, or 29 metric tons of meat per year.[20] In a single logging camp of 648 people in the Republic of Congo, the annual harvest was 8251 individual animals, equivalent to 124 tons of wild meat.[21]

Commercial logging also generates a cascade of changes within local communities that further exacerbate the impact on wildlife populations. Because wild meat has a high value per unit weight compared to other forest products, it is a valuable commodity. Other wildlife products such as horns, ivory, and skins have even greater value. Local forest communities are thus increasingly drawn into a market economy involving wildlife. Increased money allows hunters to take advantage of new hunting technologies (such as cartridges, guns, snare wires, outboard motors, and headlamps), which in turn allow more efficient harvests. Where logging activities stimulate the local economy, increased income drives up the demand for wild meat. For example, per capita harvest rates in local communities adjacent to logging roads in Congo were three to six times higher than in communities remote from such roads, and up to 75% of die meat (by weight) is sold;[21] a similar situation has been documented in Bolivian camps.[22]

Those of us concerned with tropical forests have focused on the loss of the trees and forest cover with little policy discussion of the harvest of wildlife. This has been due to a variety of factors: our cultural distaste for addressing issues involving dead animals, the moral and social complexity of a problem in which local forest people were doing much of the hunting, and the lack of information. Identifying a solution is also difficult because most of the hunting in tropical forests is not heavily capitalized or industrialized, and it is difficult to impose regulatory mechanisms on an activity that is so multifaceted and diffuse.

Where logging activities stimulate the local economy, increased income drives up the demand for wild meat.

To date, attempts to regulate the harvest of tropical forest wildlife have focused on national government attempts to regulate and educate individual hunters. However, most countries with tropical forests lack governmental institutions to manage the activities of hunters, making it impractical to control snare or shotgun use, establish hunting quotas or seasons, regulate what ages and sexes of animals are hunted, or educate individual hunters.

Regulating wildlife harvests

As commercial forestry has directly and indirectly created the conditions for increased wildlife harvests, regulatory mechanisms should focus on timber companies and forest concessionaires. In remote forest areas, these companies are almost always the only significant institutional presence and are the institutions best equipped to address the problem. National legislation has begun the process of involving logging companies in the management of wildlife populations. In Sarawak, a recent law bans all commercial trade in wildlife and wildlife products taken from the wild.[23] Although government agencies can enforce the law in urban areas, in rural areas, logging companies have been instructed to enforce the trade ban in their own concessions. They are not to allow their vehicles to carry wild meat or their staff to hunt.[24] In addition, the companies have to ensure that domestic animal protein is brought into logging camps for the workers. Similar legislation has been enacted in Bolivia,[25] and the 1996 Bolivian Forestry Law requires detailing of specific actions by logging companies, as well as the establishment of "ecological easements" and nature reserves within concessions.[26]

The industry must acknowledge that current logging practices are rarely sustainable in terms of the trees themselves, let alone in terms of the forest animals.

Although national legislation can provide both negative and positive incentives, ultimately the move toward sustainable forestry will depend on a cultural shift within the logging industry. The industry must acknowledge that current logging practices are rarely sustainable[4] in terms of the trees themselves, let alone in terms of the forest animals. If sustainable forestry is to become the conservation tool that has so often been touted, it must address the sustainability of all elements of the rainforest ecosystem.

Evidence for positive change can be found in the participation by some corporate executive officers of forestry product companies in a continuing ad hoc forum with environmental nongovernmental organizations and the World Bank.[27] "Green labeling" and independent third-party certification can provide an additional positive incentive to commercial forest managers and companies to support good practices.[28] Nevertheless, progress on a world scale has been miniscule, and in only a tiny fraction of forests presently being logged have companies demonstrated any concern for long-term stewardship of resources or for the sustainability of tropical forestry.[4]

Policy discussions and industry standards for the sustainability of tropical forestry must include consideration of wildlife. All involved must recognize that logging at almost any intensity will drive some components of rainforest biodiversity to local extinction.[29] Conservation of these elements will have to be based on areas of strict protection. If we do not see the animals for the trees, the wildlife on which both the local people and the long-term health of the forest depend will be lost.

Notes

1. N. Myers, *Conversion of Tropical Moist Forests* (National Academy Press, Washington, DC, 1980); *Forest Resource Assessment 1990: Tropical Countries* [*Forestry Paper 112,* Food and Agriculture Organization of the United Nations (UN), Rome, Italy, 1993]; *World Bank Atlas 1998* (World Bank, Washington, DC, 1998).

2. International policies supporting "sustainable" or "managed" logging include the World Conservation Strategy (1981), the Tropical Forest Action Plan (1985), the International Tropical Timber Agreement (1986), the Brundtland Commission Report (1987), Agenda 21 of the UN Conference on Environment and Development (1992), and the Convention on Biological Diversity (1993).

3. D. Ludwig, R. Hitborn, C. Walters, *Science* 260, 17 (1993); R. Rice, R. Gullison, J. Reid, *Sci. Am.* 276, 34 (April 1997).

4. I. Bowles, R. Rice, R. Mittermeier, G. Fonseca, *Science* 280, 1899 (1998).

5. T. Panayatou and P. Ashton, *Not by Timber Alone: Economics and Ecology for Sustaining Tropical Forests* (Island Press, Washington, DC, 1992); N. Johnson and B. Cabarle, *Surviving the Cut: Natural Forest Management in the Humid Tropics* [World Resources Institute (WRI), Washington, DC, 1993]; G. Hartshorn, *Ann. Rev. Ecol. Syst.* 26, 155 (1995).

6. W. Vickers, *Interciencia* 9, 366 (1984); K. Redford and J. Robinson, *Am Anthropol.* 89, 412 (1987); C. Hladik *et al.*, *Tropical Forests, People, Food: Biocultural Interactions and Applications for Development* (UN Educational, Scientific, and Cultural Organization, Paris, France, 1993).

7. J. Robinson and E. Bennett, Eds., *Hunting for Sustainability in Tropical Forests* (Columbia Univ. Press, New York, 1999).

8. Even in the absence of logging, wildlife harvesting is significant: Average rates of hunting of large mammals (>1 kg adult body mass) in tropical forests are about 6.0 animals/km^2/year in Southeast Asia (n = 2 studies), 17.5 animals/km^2/year in Africa (n = 2 studies), and 8.1 animals/km^2/year in Latin America (n = studies) [in (7)].

9. J. Robinson and K. Redford, Eds., *Neotropical Wildlife Use and Conservation* (Univ. of Chicago Press, Chicago, IL, 1991); C. Peres, *Conserv. Biol.*, in press.

10. B. Nietschmann, *Between Land and Water* (Seminar Press, New York, 1973); R. Harries and W. Vickers, *Adaptive Responses of Native Amazonians* (Academic Press, New York, 1983); K. H. Redford, R. Godshalk, K. Asher, *What About the Wild Animals? Wild Animal Species in Community Forestry in the Tropics* (Food and Agriculture Organization, Rome, 1995).

11. N. Kwapena, *Environmentalist* 4, 22 (1984); J. Brosius, *Sarawak Mus. J.* 36 (no. 57, new series), 173 (1986).

12. A. Stearman, in (7).

13. K. Redford, *BioScience*, 42, 412 (1992); J. Robinson and R. Bodmer, *J. Wildl. Manage.* 63, 1 (1999).

14. J. Mills and P. Jackson, *Killed for a Cure: A Review of the Worldwide Trade in Tiger Bone* (Traffic International, Cambridge, 1994); S. Nash, *Still in Business: The Ivory Trade in Asia, Seven Years after the CITES Ban* (Traffic International, Cambridge, 1997); Ape Alliance, *The African Bushmeat Trade—A Recipe for Extinction* (Ape Alliance, London, 1998).

15. M. Powers *et al.*, *BioScience*, 46, 609 (1996).

16. H. Howe and G. Vande Kerckhove, *Ecology* 62, 1093 (1981); A. Gautier-Hion *et al.*, *Oecologia* 65, 324 (1985); M. Willson, A. Irvine, N. Walsh, *Biotropica* 21, 133 (1989); C. Tutin, E. Williamson, M. Rogers, M. Fernandez, *J. Trop. Ecol.* 7, 181 (1991).

17. T. Whitmore and J. Sayer, in *Tropical Deforestation and Species Extinction,* T. Whitmore and J. Sayer, Eds. (Chapman & Hall, London, 1992); WRI, *World Resources 1994–1995* (Oxford Univ. Press, New York, 1994).

18. In Asia, Africa, and Latin America, an estimated 58, 19, and 28%, respectively, has already been logged by commercial enterprises [A. Grieser Johns, *Timber Production and Biodiversity Conservation in Tropical Rain Forests* (Cambridge Univ. Press, Cambridge, 1997)].

19. D. Wilkie and J. Carpenter, *The Impact of Bushmeat Hunting on Forest Fauna and Local Economies in the Congo Basin* (unpublished report, WCS, Bronx, NY, 1998).

20. WCS/Sarawak Forest Department, *A Master Plan for Wildlife in Sarawak* (Sarawak Forest Department, Kuching, Sarawak, Malaysia, 1996).

21. P. Auzel and D. Witkie, in (7).

22. D. Guinart, *Los Mamiferos del Bosque Sernideciduo Neotropical de Lomerio (Bolivia). Interacción Indigena,* thesis, Universitat de Barcelona (1997); D. Rumiz and L. Solar, *La caza, su impacto y aporte económico en una concesión forestal del Bajo Paraguá* (BOLFOR, Santa Cruz, Bolivia, 1996).

23. State Government of Sarawak, *Wild Life Protection Ordinance,* Sarawak Government Gazette, Vol. VI (NS), No. 2 (1998).

24. Rural communities and their leaders have given strong support to the trade ban because hunting for subsistence is still allowed and they see these measures as conserving their wildlife resources [State Government of Sarawak, *Proceedings of the Dewan Undangan Negeri, First Sitting* (Kuching, Sarawak Malaysia, 1998)].

25. Government of Bolivia, *Historical Ecological Pause* and its regulations (DS 22407, La Paz, Bolivia, 1990).

26. Government of Bolivia, *Forestry Law 1700* and its regulations (DS 24453, La Paz, Bolivia, 1996).

27. Some companies are actively collaborating with conservation programs to establish best practices for wildlife management on concessions—for example, the Congolaise Industrielle des Bois in Congo and the Samling Strategic Corporation in Sarawak are collaborating with WCS field programs. Another encouraging sign is an initiative involving the World Wildlife Fund (WWF) and the World Bank that promotes sustainable commercial forestry [*The World Bank/WWF Alliance for Forest Conservation and Sustainable Use,* fact sheet, 29 April 1998].

28. V. Viana *et al., Certification of Forest Products: Issues and Perspectives* (Island Press, Washington, DC, 1996); Forest Stewardship Council, *Principles and Criteria for Forest Management* (Oaxaca, Mexico, 1996).

29. P. Frumhoff, *BioScience,* 45, 456 (1995); I. Noble and R. Dirzo, *Science* 277, 522 (1997); K. Bawa and R. Seidler, *Conserv. Biol.* 12, 46 (1998).

30. Funding was provided in part by the U.S. Agency for International Development, the Art Ortenberg/Liz Claiborne Foundation in Bolivia and Congo, and the John D. and Catherine T. MacArthur Foundation in Sarawak. We especially thank the state government of Sarawak for supporting our collaborative efforts.

6

Oil Companies Pose a Threat to the Rain Forests

Joe Kane

Joe Kane, an award-winning author and journalist, has been reporting on the Amazon since 1985.

Oil companies are pushing deeper and deeper into the Amazon rain forest in search of oil. In the process, they are polluting the forest, creeks, and rivers with toxic waste and thereby threatening the health, crops, and hunting and fishing lands of the indigenous people who call the forest their home. Due to a lack of legal protections, local tribes have begun to resist the intrusion of oil companies into their territories by means of protests and acts of industrial sabotage.

Deep in the Ecuadorian Amazon rain forest, in a village more than a hundred miles from the nearest road, a young Cofan Indian named Bolivar smiles as he describes the day that his people finally stood up to their most powerful enemy—the oil companies.

The Cofan had always depended on the rain forest for everything—their food, clothing, and homes. Then, in 1972, Texaco began extracting oil from the Cofan homeland. Over the next 20 years, Texaco dumped billions of gallons of untreated toxic oil waste directly into the forest, creeks, and rivers on which the Cofan depended for their survival.

"Texaco poisoned everything," Bolivar says. He and his family and friends fled deeper into the forest. There they lived as before, until one day in November of 1991, when 24 employees of an American oil-exploration company marched into their new village and started cutting trees. The Cofan decided that they had had enough. "We had nowhere left to run," Bolivar says. "We had to fight back."

They took the oil workers prisoner and marched them out of the forest at spear point. They burned an oil well and destroyed a helicopter landing pad. When the Ecuadorian government sent in soldiers, the Cofan faced them down and backed them off. But the Cofan didn't stop there. They and 30,000 other residents of the Oriente (ore-ee-EN-tay), as

Reprinted from Joe Kane, "Battle for the Rain Forest," *Scholastic Update,* February 8, 1999. Copyright © 1999 by Scholastic Inc. Reprinted by permission of Scholastic Inc.

the Ecuadorian Amazon is known, brought a lawsuit against Texaco, demanding more than a billion dollars for ruining their health, crops, and hunting and fishing lands. Filed in federal court in White Plains, New York, where Texaco has its headquarters, the suit poses a fundamental question: Should American environmental and human-rights standards apply to U.S. companies operating overseas?

No laws protect the tribes

The suit has the potential to force U.S. oil companies to change the way they do business not only in Ecuador, but throughout the Amazon and, indeed, the world. Foreign oil now accounts for more than half the energy used in the United States, and giants such as Mobil, Occidental, Arco, and Oryx are pushing ever deeper into native territory in Venezuela, Colombia, Peru, and Ecuador. Under the laws of most South American countries, the native, or indigenous, people have no legal right to the oil beneath their homelands and no say in how it is extracted. Nor, for all practical purposes, are there any laws that control the environmental and human-rights consequences of oil production.

Increasingly, indigenous tribes that find themselves in the same predicament as the Cofan are taking matters into their own hands. In Peru, Machiguenga Indians recently forced Royal Dutch/Shell to abandon plans to develop a natural-gas field. In Colombia, the U'wa people threatened mass suicide if Occidental drilled for oil on their lands; in the face of worldwide negative publicity, Occidental recently scaled back its plans. In Ecuador, where the government has leased 85 percent of Amazon lands occupied by indigenous people to oil companies, Quichua Indians armed with machetes and shotguns have shut down Arco wells. The Achuar are also battling Arco. And the Huaorani people—who are threatened with eradication of their culture for the sake of enough oil to meet U.S. energy needs for 10 days—have marched on Maxus Energy facilities.

Texaco poisoned everything.

These, however, are isolated battles in a much larger war. More typical is the agreement between Occidental and the Secoya, a tiny and isolated tribe. In exchange for signing a contract that enables the company to extract 155 million barrels of oil, Occidental gave the Secoya three stoves, three water pumps, some roofing material, an outboard motor, and three first-aid kits. Critics denounced the deal as "beads and trinkets," but the oil company defended it, saying the Secoya "have a very clear picture of what they want."

As they battle the oil companies, the indigenous people also find themselves battling national governments. Most of these countries are impoverished and desperately need the oil revenue. In Ecuador, where 79 percent of the population lives in poverty, the government depends on oil for nearly half its revenues.

Nowhere are the consequences of this dilemma more profound than among the Cofan. When Texaco started taking oil out of the Oriente, it drilled 339 wells, blasted 18,000 miles of trails with dynamite, and cut 300 miles of roads. It built a pipeline that ruptured constantly, spilling more oil into the forest than was spilled in the worst ecological disaster in U.S. history, when the oil tanker Exxon Valdez ran aground off the coast of Alaska in 1989.

The use of substandard practices

Texaco and its partner, Petroecuador, also dug hundreds of waste pits, into which they poured nearly all the toxic waste from the oil-extraction process, a practice that has long been outlawed in most of the U.S. The pits regularly leaked and washed out in the Oriente's heavy rains. By 1992, they had discharged more than 30 billion gallons of untreated waste directly into the creeks, rivers, and lakes that are the primary sources of drinking, bathing, and fishing water for the local people. When a team of researchers analyzed these waters in 1993, they found extremely high levels of poisons. These poisons are considered so deadly, that the U.S. Environmental Protection Agency says any amount at all poses a serious cancer risk.

Critics charge that Texaco deliberately used substandard practices to maximize profits.

Texaco says it broke no laws and has paid Ecuador $40 million for clean-up efforts. D. York LeCorgne, a former president of Texaco's Ecuadorian operations, says the waste pits "are not an inherent cause of pollution" and that pipeline spills were caused by acts of nature. According to LeCorgne, the company complied not only with Ecuadorian law, "but also with oil-industry standards of best practice and our own guiding principles and objectives, which affirm our commitment to the environment."

Critics charge that Texaco deliberately used substandard practices to maximize profits. The company broke no laws, they say, only because there were virtually no laws to break. On paper, Ecuador has laws that protect the Amazon's nature reserves, national parks, and indigenous people. But oil companies have told the government they won't tolerate any laws that might impede production, and the government has not enforced them. Furthermore, in a country considered one of the world's most corrupt, most of its oil revenues were allowed to be siphoned off by the oil companies and the small elite that controls the country.

Poisonous sludge

On a recent trip to the old Cofan hunting grounds, Bolivar points out a rusting metal pipe discharging poisonous sludge from a nearby oil well into a creek. The banks are coated with a film of oil, the trees along it are brown and lifeless, and the water itself smells like tar. Throughout the forest, dozens of creeks and lakes are in similar condition. Traditionally, the Cofan survived by hunting and gathering, and by growing a few staples such as bananas and manioc. Their relationship with the forest was complex and highly sensitive—to make a blowgun and darts for hunting, for example, required more than 60 distinct forest products. But once Texaco came, Bolivar says, "we starved." He vividly recalls the day he managed to hunt and kill a sort of wild pig called a peccary, "but it was so soaked with oil that we could not eat it. We knew then that if we did not leave, we would die."

In biological terms, the Oriente is one of the richest places in the world; though no larger than Alabama, it is believed to be home to some 5 percent of all the species on the planet. In a single plot the size of two football fields, for example, researchers have identified 246 species of trees, more than are native to all of Western Europe. If cures for diseases such as AIDS and cancer were ever discovered, some researchers say, chances are they will come from the Oriente or from the Amazonian region that surrounds it.

Vast regions of the Oriente have already been destroyed, without any protection for their biological treasures.

But as the Oriente is opened up for oil development, it suffers not only from long-term pollution but from deforestation. Poor settlers from other parts of the country follow the oil roads into the rain forest, where they earn free title to land by "improving" it—in other words, by cutting down the trees and turning rain forest into farms. Often, these are lands that have long been occupied by indigenous people. Vast regions of the Oriente have already been destroyed, without any protection for their biological treasures.

Royal Dutch/Shell is expected to open an oil concession on the eastern side of the new Cofan lands, and Bolivar has little doubt that another round of confrontations will soon begin.

"We have no choice," he says. "This is our home." But as he has also come to learn, however painfully, it is a home intimately connected to a distant nation whose thirst for oil is second to none.

7

Fragmentation Is a Threat to the Rain Forests

William F. Laurance

William F. Laurance is a senior research scientist at the National Institute for Research in the Amazon, located in Manaus, Brazil.

Logging, development, and farming in the rain forests leave the forests divided into fragments. Research shows that forest fragments under a certain size are unable to maintain the structure of the original forest. Fragmentation kills trees on a massive scale, and those within a few hundred yards of the forest edges are especially vulnerable. It is reported that up to 36 percent of the biomass in forest fragments will be lost soon after being isolated from surrounding forest. In order to help save the rain forest from further destruction, advocates need to educate the public about plant products, boycott corporations that exploit the rain forest, and lobby government leaders to support rain forest conservation.

To Portuguese explorers of the sixteenth century, the rainforest of the Amazon was a vast, verdant hell. But they pressed forward eagerly in search of gold and rare woods, while missionaries looked for heathen souls for conversion to Christianity. Soon after Europeans claimed the land, they established plantations and enslaved thousands of Indians to work them.

Historically, the Amazonian rainforest remained nearly intact because of its sheer size, its soils that were unsuitable for agriculture, and the deterrent of such endemic diseases as malaria and yellow fever. Recently, however, the tide has turned against one of the last great forested areas remaining in a largely deforested world. In the Brazilian Amazon, annual forest loss from all causes rose from less than 3 million acres in 1991 to an average of 4.8 million acres during each of the past three years [1995–1997]—the equivalent of seven football fields a minute. In 1995 alone, more than 7 million acres were destroyed—an area roughly the size of Belgium.

Reprinted from William F. Laurance, "Fragments of the Forest," with permission from *Natural History*, July/August 1998. Copyright the American Museum of Natural History, 1998.

Logging threat

Using chain saws and bulldozers, industrial loggers go after such valuable timber trees as mahogany, but they also kill many other kinds of trees in the process. In logged areas, up to half of the protective canopy is destroyed, drying out the remaining forest and increasing the likelihood of fires. Loggers also create roads, opening up forest tracts for settlers who clear plots for farming or cattle raising, and for hunters who slaughter peccaries, tapirs, monkeys, and jaguars.

Companies from Malaysia, Indonesia, China, South Korea, and Singapore are stripping the Amazon's most valuable timber in record time. Their major customers are the United States, Europe, and Japan. In 1996 alone, Asian companies invested more than half a billion dollars in the Brazilian timber industry, and they now own or control more than 30 million acres of rainforest in Brazil, Suriname, and Guyana. Until recently, major deforestation was concentrated along the southeastern arc of the Amazon—in the Brazilian states of Acre, Rondônia, Mato Grosso, and Pará, as well as in Bolivia.

Development threat

But now new roads have been cut into the heart of the Amazon Basin, providing access to areas once considered too remote for development. One such highway runs from the city of Manaus, in the central Amazon, 600 miles north to the Venezuelan border. In 1997, Brazilian president Fernando Cardoso announced that approximately 15 million acres of forest along the highway would be opened to settlement, creating a farming area "so colossal that it would double the nation's agricultural production." Large expanses of forest have already been cleared along fifty miles of the new road.

With a burgeoning population that now exceeds 1.5 million, Manaus is the hub of development in the Amazon. Home to the infamous "rubber barons" at the turn of the century, Manaus was, for a few brief decades, one of the world's wealthiest cities, where legendary high-rollers flaunted their wealth by lighting cigars with paper currency and sending their soiled laundry to Europe. A grand opera house still stands as a testament to its past opulence. The rubber boom that fueled the city's rise collapsed long ago, but today, money and people are again pouring into the city as tropical timber is converted into cold cash.

Forest fragments are threatened

Logged and fragmented forests—and the scrubby regrowth that colonizes unused fields and pastures—are far more prone to fires than are intact rainforests. And since the traditional method of clearing land is to hack down vegetation and then burn what remains, the danger is ever present that farmers' fires will rage out of control—especially in drought years. According to archaeologists who have studied charcoal deposits in Amazonian soils, four catastrophic fires during the past 2,000 years coincided with droughts caused by El Niño. Now, even minor droughts have catastrophic potential. In the first three months of 1998, in the northern

Brazilian state of Roraima, fires lit by farmers and ranchers swept through more than 2 million acres of savanna and deciduous forest. In Manaus, the smoke from fires lit in local forests became so severe that the airport was temporarily closed and hospitals reported a 40 percent rise in the incidence of respiratory problems.

Decades ago, when ecologists and other life scientists realized that this kind of development would inevitably reduce and fragment the Amazonian forest, they began to wonder if any plants and animals could withstand such an onslaught. If reserves were to be set aside, how large would they need to be to ensure the survival of rainforest species into the next century?

Studying the effects of fragmentation

With such questions in mind, ornithologist Thomas Lovejoy initiated the Minimum Critical Size of Ecosystems Project in 1979. (Some years later, it was renamed the Biological Dynamics of Forest Fragments Project.) Lovejoy was soon joined by fellow ornithologist Richard Bierregaard and several Brazilian colleagues in what was to become one of the world's longest-running ecological experiments. Their efforts were facilitated by a Brazilian law stipulating that 50 percent of the land in any Amazonian development project must be retained as uncut forest. After learning that four experimental cattle ranches were to be sponsored by the Brazilian government near Manaus, Lovejoy proposed that the ranchers divide the required portion of uncut forest into isolated patches of various sizes, ranging from 2.5 to 25,000 acres. Researchers could then study the communities of trees, birds, mammals, frogs, butterflies, and other animals in the areas, both before and after creation of the patches, to learn how each was affected by fragmentation.

But the plans for the project soon had to be modified. Fragment placement was reorganized because official maps did not accurately reflect the topography. Trucks bogged down in rivers of mud. Fieldworkers suffered from local diseases. And the project's botanists were overwhelmed by the stunning diversity of the Amazonian forest: they encountered more than a thousand species of trees.

Logged and fragmented forests—and the scrubby regrowth that colonizes unused fields and pastures—are far more prone to fires than are intact rainforests.

Still, the project survived and grew. As word spread, researchers from Brazil, the United States, England, and Canada arrived and initiated new studies. Project scientists trained dozens of Brazilian graduate students, several of whom later joined the project's research staff. Under its current scientific coordinator, Claude Gascon, new research avenues are being initiated, and an outreach program is helping to educate decision makers about forest management.

While the project has not achieved all its ambitious objectives, it has provided vital insights into the responses of ecosystems to fragmentation.

My own team is trying to learn how trees and lianas (woody vines) are affected. We work in permanent plots (each 2.5 acres) located in fragments ranging from 2.5 to 250 acres, as well as in nearby continuous forest. In all, our plots contain more than 57,000 trees. In the early 1980s, agile field technicians climbed thousands of these trees to collect leaves or flowers for identification; many were new to science. We return to our plots every few years to remeasure the trees and lianas and to count the dead, damaged, and new trees to determine which species are increasing or declining.

Fragmentation kills

We have found that rainforests have their own unique rhythm and that fragmentation completely changes it. In continuous forests, trees die and fall at a slow, regular rate. The falling trees create small openings in the dense forest canopy, which are soon resealed by the growth of new vegetation. Like a protective skin, the continuous canopy maintains the rainforest interior's cool, shady, and humid conditions, upon which many species of specialized plants and animals depend. Fragmentation kills trees on a massive scale, and those within a few hundred yards of forest edges are especially vulnerable. The dry heat of the surrounding pastures penetrates the fragments, killing some trees, many of which die standing. Lifeless limbs break off under their own weight, sometimes dangling from tangled vines in the canopy. These suspended limbs, some weighing hundreds of pounds, can fall at any time. (They have been aptly named widow-makers.) Winds accelerate over the surrounding denuded pastures, then slam into the fragments, sometimes toppling trees like dominoes and shearing off limbs and crowns.

We have found that rainforests have their own unique rhythm and that fragmentation completely changes it.

These changes make Swiss cheese of the once-continuous canopy. Tree species specifically adapted to the rainforest interior die or shed their leaves, while vines, lianas, and weeds may increase in abundance. The complex architecture of the forest—from the ground to the treetops—is markedly altered. If, over time, plant communities in forest fragments become skewed toward a few species that thrive in the new conditions, those that are specialized for life in the deep, continuous forest may disappear. Three-quarters of all rainforest tree species are rare in the first place; only a few individuals can be found in a hundred acres. Many problems, such as those caused by inbreeding and genetic drift, plague these small populations and often drive them to extinction. In isolated fragments, entire populations may be extirpated. The overall result is likely to be a major loss of plant diversity.

What's more, many plants require specific animals—insects, birds, bats, or monkeys—to transfer their pollen or disperse their seeds. Every species of orchid, for example, is pollinated by a particular type of bee, while each fig has its own special wasp pollinator. Fragmentation affects many kinds of organisms. If a crucial pollinator or seed-disperser disappears from a fragment, dependent plant species may rapidly go extinct. Such ripple effects will further diminish the biological diversity in forest that has been broken up for timber, ranching, and farming. Our research has revealed an alarming and unanticipated phenomenon: the sudden collapse in the total amount of living material, or biomass, in forest fragments. Small patches lose up to 36 percent of their biomass soon after being isolated from surrounding forest, a process that begins when large trees near fragment edges die.

Biomass loss within fragments will probably cause additional gas emissions that are the equivalent of destroying an additional 1 to 3 million acres of rainforest each year.

This loss has important implications for the global climate. One of the principal causes of the greenhouse effect, aside from the burning of fossil fuels, is the rapid destruction of forests. As trees and other plants are burned or decomposed by microbes, they release huge amounts of carbon dioxide, methane, and nitrous oxide into the atmosphere, increasing the greenhouse effect. Our findings reveal that biomass loss within fragments will probably cause additional gas emissions that are the equivalent of destroying an additional 1 to 3 million acres of rainforest each year.

How to save the rainforests

How can we help save the rainforests? We can support efforts to slow the world's burgeoning population. We can support organizations such as the Rainforest Action Network and Rainforest Alliance, which promote forest protection in the developing world. We can educate the public about plant products—from picture frames to furniture—that are manufactured from endangered species. We can boycott corporations that aggressively exploit the rainforest and can lobby our leaders to support rainforest conservation.

And we can fight for the forests in our own backyards. In developing countries like Brazil, conservationists from wealthy countries are understandably seen as hypocrites. In addition to consuming rainforest products, industrialized countries continue to destroy their own old-growth forests. Why should Brazilians protect their forests when the rich countries of the world are unwilling to do the same?

Destruction of the Amazon Rain Forest Threatens Global Climate

Peter Bunyard

Peter Bunyard is the science editor of the Ecologist *magazine and the author of* The Breakdown of Climate.

The destruction of Earth's rain forests, in particular the Amazon, will have a devastating effect on global climate. Since rain forests absorb carbon dioxide (CO_2), when they are destroyed by fires or logging, they add to the concentration of carbon dioxide in the atmosphere. This CO_2 contributes to global warming. The Amazon rain forest also serves as a heat pump, transferring solar energy from the tropics to northern latitudes. Destruction of the rain forest will be responsible for collapsing this energy-transfer mechanism and possibly causing a significant cooling over temperate zone countries such as Britain while causing the Amazon to heat up significantly. This alteration of the climate system will also lead to the generation of strong, turbulent jet streams of air in the mid and high latitudes. In addition, deforestation of rain forests will have a major impact on the distribution of water, which could lead to an increase in flooding, "sandification," and erosion.

The Amazon Basin plays a number of key, often neglected roles—including that of a giant 'heat-pump' that sends energy from the Tropics into the colder high latitudes—that produce a climate in which we can live. But at the current rate of destruction, much of the Amazon rainforest will be gone in a few decades.

What would have seemed obvious to any clear-thinking ecologist is now becoming disturbingly apparent: the destruction of the world's great tropical rainforests, and that of the Amazon in particular, will have a devastating effect on climate. It represents a veritable triple whammy: first by turning a net carbon sink [absorber of carbon dioxide] into a source; second, by throwing a spanner in the works of an extraordinary heat-pump that gives the people of Northern Europe a climate in which they can live;

Reprinted from Peter Bunyard, "Eradicating the Amazon Rain Forest Will Wreak Havoc on Climate," *The Ecologist*, March/April 1999, with permission. Web site: http://www.theecologist.org.

and third, by causing tropical ecosystems to collapse, as the ecological base provided by the intact forest system and vital for forest regeneration is destroyed, with all that means for agriculture across Latin America, in South-east Asia and Africa.

Carbon emissions from forest destruction

The tropical forests of Central and South America are unique among tropical forests in the world in their capacity to grow, even when seemingly mature. Oliver Phillips and his colleagues report in *Science*[1] that they have measured as much as one tonne per hectare per year of growth in such intact forests. Consequently, one of Phillips' colleagues, John Grace from the University of Edinburgh, estimates that if all the forests of the Brazilian Amazon, covering some 360 million hectares, put on biomass in that way, the Amazon in Brazil alone would be an annual sink of up to 0.56 billion tonnes of carbon.[2]

When forest destruction takes place, however, that significant sink becomes a net source. Carbon release as forests get destroyed is what ecologists and environmentalists have, for the most part, focussed on in gauging the impact of tropical forest destruction on the world's climate, pointing out the obvious fact that such releases add to total emissions of carbon dioxide to the atmosphere. Much of the time they have wrangled over the exact rate of destruction and the amounts of carbon released—anywhere from 0.5 to 4 billion tons of carbon per year from forest destruction worldwide, but mostly in the Tropics. If the figure of nearly 9 million hectares of tropical forest destroyed by fire worldwide during 1998 is correct, then, on the basis that a hectare of tropical rainforest contains between 100 and 250 tonnes of carbon in its biomass and three-quarters of the total burns or decomposes, the carbon emissions will have totalled between one and two billion tonnes from that source alone—equivalent to one-third of the emissions from fossil fuel burning across the world. To make matters worse, when areas are cleared of trees the surrounding forest suffers die-back and disintegration. Carbon emissions from areas of the Amazon that have been cleared are likely to be at least seven per cent higher than previously thought because of that die-back—the equivalent of felling one million more hectares than are actually felled.[3]

The Amazon as heat-pump for northern Europe at stake

Whilst the impact of tropical forest destruction on the uptake of carbon has now been modelled, rarely have climatologists taken into account a potentially more important and devastating consequence of the destruction of tropical rainforests: the process by which heat over the Tropics is carried away in massive rain clouds and distributed by means of the mass circulation of air towards the cooler, higher latitude regions. That way the energy of the Sun some 2.5 times greater annually over the Equator than the Poles gets evened out over the entire planet. We are now discovering that without that intact forest, the energy-transfer mechanism could collapse. Climate models, however, do not take this into account. In treating ecology as a set of disconnected processes, we have obstinately shut our eyes to the extraordinary inter connectedness of life on this planet and its role in generating climate. Nothing better exemplifies the single process of climate and ecology than the rainforests of the Amazon Basin.

All tropical forests contribute to the process of energy transfer, but of all the regions of tropical rainforests, the Amazon is by far the most important by dint of its sheer size—some seven million square kilometres in total. Any reduction in the mass movement of water vapour as a result of rainforest destruction will perturb climate every bit as powerfully as the addition of greenhouse gases.

According to the Brazilian physicist, Eneas Salati, between 50 and 75 per cent of all the water falling as rain over the Amazon is evaporated and transpired back into the atmosphere, from where it falls again as the Trade Winds blowing across the tropical Atlantic Ocean deposit it up to seven times across the entire 4,000 kilometre expanse of the Amazon Basin in an extraordinary and unparalleled leap frogging.[4]

All tropical forests contribute to the process of energy transfer, but of all the regions of tropical rainforests, the Amazon is by far the most important by dint of its sheer size.

In a healthy rainforest, transpiration, by which vegetation pumps water through its stomata into the atmosphere, accounts for 60 per cent of the humidity in the air over central Amazonia and evaporation from the leaves and stems of vegetation for the remaining 40 per cent. When the forest is intact virtually no evaporation occurs from the soil, but rather directly from the above-ground biomass, therefore from the stems and leaves of the vegetation. That evapotranspiration constitutes enormous quantities of solar energy and according to the Brazilian climatologist, Luiz Carlos Molion,[5] takes up as much as 80 per cent of all the energy directed down over the forests from the Sun. Salati estimates that the energy flow across the Amazon Basin is equivalent to 5 to 6 million atom bombs exploding every day. Over the intact forest, with its powerful evapotranspiration pump, 75 per cent of that energy is used to evaporate water. The hot, humid air generated over the rainforest then rises rapidly and develops into cumulo-nimbus thunder-clouds that simultaneously water areas further downwind and release the energy bound up as 'latent heat' back into the atmosphere. There it drives the great air masses that are carried aloft in the atmosphere travelling west across the Amazon Basin until they hit the mountain chain of the Andes. The flow then splits into three branches. The central part jumps over the mountains into the Pacific and continues west along the Equator, following the convergence of the warm northern sea current; the southern stream is deflected by the Andes and passes over Patagonia via the Brazilian cerrado (savanna) while the northern stream, carried aloft in the circulation of the air mass between the equator and the upper reaches of the tropics—the Hadley Circulation, as it is referred to—crosses the Caribbean, touches the eastern seaboard of the US and goes over the Atlantic towards northern Europe.

However, without the intact forest, the amount of solar energy that can be carried away towards the higher latitudes is cut by a fifth or more.

Just that cut alone could be sufficient to cause a significant cooling over temperate zone countries such as Britain in the north Atlantic. Combined with a seizing-up of the Gulf Stream, that loss in heat transfer would be a devastating blow to the climate of northern Europe and Scandinavia.

Moreover, as a result of improved modelling it now appears that the changes in the energy transfer from the tropics to the subtropics brought about through destruction of the Amazon rainforest will, in the mid and high latitudes, lead to the generation of strong, turbulent, jet streams of air (Rossby Waves) that drive like a wedge between the major circulation cells of the global circulatory system.[6]

We should be warned: the last glaciation was associated with an Amazon Basin virtually devoid of human tropical rainforests.

The polar front jet stream, the most northerly branch of the Rossby Wave, is the most powerful of all the jet streams. It drives between the air masses that form in the polar region and those which form between the tropics and the temperate zone. It therefore cuts its way at high speed between the warm air of the tropics and the cold air of the North Pole. Just how far south that jet stream pushes makes all the difference to the weather. When it pushes south it brings cold, dry bracing air with it. When it retreats northwards, then we get the warm, water-laden air of the tropics with all that entails in terms of heavy rainfall, high surface winds and atmospheric depression. The further south the polar jet stream pushes, the colder the weather. If the Hadley Circulation becomes weaker because it has gathered less energy because of deforestation, then the jet stream will have more push and power to force the entire weather system of the northern hemisphere down towards the equator. That will mean less rain and more cold over the temperate zone. That shift, closely linked as it would be with the weakening of the Hadley Circulation and combined with a seizing-up of the Gulf Stream, would clearly play havoc with Britain and northern Europe's weather.

We in Britain currently have to thank those jet streams for making our weather system so extraordinarily variable with its fluctuations between wet, gusty south-westerlies and the cold, bracing air that sweeps down from the Arctic. Indeed, a change in what happens to the jet stream, because of deforestation over the Amazon, could be sufficient to plunge us into a weather regime such as we have not seen for thousands of years. We should be warned: the last glaciation was associated with an Amazon Basin virtually devoid of humid tropical rainforests.

Just a 10 or 20 per cent drop in the amount of water vapour being carried in the system makes a substantial difference to the total energy flow—a reduction equivalent in energy terms to more than 20 times the total energy used in industry and agriculture across the entire planet. Relatively small changes in energy build-up in the Pacific Ocean can cause a climate system to switch, just like the 1997/98 El Nino. That should give us cause for reflection on what we are doing to the Amazon as well as to the tropical forests of other regions of the planet.

Baking the Amazon Basin

Forest destruction is also likely to have severe local impacts. If a significant proportion of the forest is destroyed—perhaps little more than that already gone—the system of heat transfer will begin to collapse, both because the leap-frogging of the water cycle across the Amazon Basin needs the intact forest to fuel it through evapotranspiration and will therefore run out of 'steam'; and second, with less water vapour in the clouds, less energy will get carried away to the higher latitudes. The ultimate consequence is that the Amazon Basin will heat up and begin to bake, with inevitable impact on the soil, while equally the higher latitudes will cool.

That view is corroborated by the work of J. Lean and P. R. Rowntree of the UK Met Office who find from their improved models that deforestation over the Brazilian Amazon could lead to rainfall over the Colombian Andes, during certain seasons, falling by as much as 65 per cent. That fall would be drastic for agriculture. They also corroborate Salati's contention that the regrowth of forest within areas that have been cleared of forest, as well as the survival of forest in outlying areas, are likely to be threatened by an extended dry season combined with less rainfall at other times of the year.[7]

When the forest is cleared, the contrast between day and night temperatures becomes more extreme.

Deforestation clearly has a major and immediate impact on the distribution of water. A 350-hectare tea plantation in tropical Africa showed a two-fold increase in moderate flooding and a four-fold increase in more serious flooding compared with the nearby natural forest. Molion points out that the Amazon forest canopy intercepts on average about 15 per cent of the rainfall and that its removal would lead to as much as 4,000 cubic metres (tonnes) per hectare per year hitting the ground. Because of soil compaction much of that water would run off directly into the rivers rather than being retained and maintaining some soil moisture. The net result would be 'sandification' whereby the heavy drops of rain hitting the ground cause the selective erosion of finer clay particles, leaving behind increasingly coarse sand. With time, the remaining 'soil' would have virtually no water-retaining properties and the forest would be unable to regenerate itself. Soil under intact forest absorbs ten times more water compared with nearby areas that have had pasture for five years. Outside the forest and away from its soil-protecting attributes, erosion increases a thousand-fold.[8]

Moreover, when the forest is cleared, the contrast between day and night temperatures becomes more extreme, so leading to gustier winds that dry out soils and send dust swirling into the air. Even if some forest is left around the edges of clearings it will be under siege from water-stress as the water table plummets. Large areas of the Amazon Basin are far closer to water-stress than scientists once thought and the clear cutting and burning of large areas of rainforest would inevitably precipitate dieback and death of the nearby forest.

We have no idea just what proportion of forest must be left for the system to be self-maintaining. It may be three-quarters; perhaps even less: if so, with 20 per cent already gone, we are terrifyingly close to those limits. How ludicrous then to propose, as the presidents of the World Bank, the World Wide Fund for Nature (WWF) and Brazil did in February 1998, saving 10 per cent of the Brazilian Amazon, which would be nowhere near adequate.

Accelerating destruction

The terrifying fact is that tropical forests are being destroyed across the planet at accelerating rates. Current estimates indicate that as much as 17 million hectares of tropical forests are being destroyed each year, with up to six million hectares alone of that destruction taking place in the Brazilian Amazon, when destruction from charcoal manufacture for pig-iron production is also taken into account.[10] Quite aside from charcoal production, more than 50 million hectares of the Brazilian Amazon have gone in a matter of a few decades: if so, that would entail a loss the size of France and one-sixth of the total three and a half million square kilometres of Brazil's rainforest.[11, 12]

Deforestation in the states of Para and Maranhao to the north of the Amazon and on the eastern plains has been continuing inexorably. By the end of 1988, as much as 21 million hectares had gone. Just a decade later the total was 27.5 million hectares, an area greater than the UK. That is the official figure; on the other hand, the government has been minimising the impact of the charcoal-fired pig-iron industry which has increased six-fold over the past eight years to a production of more than 1.5 million tons.[13] Deforestation in the state of Para may therefore be much worse.[14] According to the former Brazilian minister for the environment, Jose Lutzenberger, when all destruction in those two states is taken into account, the remaining forest there may well be gone in a matter of years. The destruction of rainforest in the states of Acre and Rondonia has been equally severe and, after gold was discovered in the Yanomami lands of Roraima, has now spread there like a cancer. In 1998, in part because of the exceptionally strong El Nino, but equally because of drying out through deforestation, unprecedented fires raged in the natural standing forest in Roraima. The forest is dying in front of our very eyes.

With the Amazon rainforest destroyed, the world will discover too late that it has pulled down one of the most important underpinnings of a stable, global climate.

Yet international financial institutions and governments still actively promote heavily-subsidised forest destruction. Everywhere, the International Monetary Fund (IMF) is forcing governments of Third World debtor countries to cash in their forests in order to maximise foreign exchange earnings so that Western bankers may be paid their due.[15] The Brazilian government, for instance, under its President Fernando Henrique Cardoso, has recently launched a new aggressive programme of selling off Brazil's patrimony of natural resources to foreign investors. As a result of the new structural adjustment plan imposed by the IMF, Brazil has had to agree to cut its budget for environmental issues by 66 per cent and has even been forced to give up its plan to spend 1.5 million US dollars for the protection of just 10 per cent of the Brazilian Amazon.

It is a scandal that the forests of Amazonia and the rest of the world, which provide us with so many irreplaceable social and ecological services and which, not least, play such a critical role in assuring climatic stability, should be annihilated for short-term cash gains. With the Amazon rainforest destroyed, the world will discover too late that it has pulled down one of the most important underpinnings of a stable, global climate.

Notes

1. Oliver Phillips et al., Changes in the Carbon Balance of Tropical Forests: Evidence from Long-Term Plots, *Science*, Vol. 282 16 Oct., 1998.

2. J. Grace, Forests and the Global Carbon Cycle. *S. It. E. Atti*, 1996, 17:7–11.

3. William Laurence, *Science*. Vol. 27. p. 1117.

4. Eneas Salati, The Forest and the Hydrological Cycle, in *The Geophysiology of Amazonia*. ed. Robert Dickinson, Wiley, 1987.

5. Carlos Molion, *The Ecologist*. Vol. 19. No. 6, 1989.

6. H. Zhang, K. McGuffie and A. Henderson-Sellers, Impacts of Tropical Deforestation. Part II: The Role of Large-Scale Dynamics. American Meteorological Society, *Journal of Climate*, Vol. 9, p. 2498.

7. J. Lean and P.R. Rowntree, A GCM simulation of the impact of Amazonian deforestation on climate using an improved canopy representation, *Q. J. R. Meteorol. Soc.* 119, pp. 509–530.

8. Harald Sioli, The Effects of Deforestation in Amazonia. *The Ecologist*, Vol. 17, No. 4/5, 1987.

9. *The Ecologist*, Vol. 17, No. 4/5, 1987.

10. Charcoal production for pig-iron manufacture in the States of Para and Maranhao has steadily increased and in 1998 pig-iron exports from Amazonia may top 1,500,000 tons, six-fold up from 260,000 tons in 1990. That manufacture requires some 3.9 million hectares of forest a year.

11. Jose Carlos Carvalho, *Amazonia: Heaven of a New World*. Editora Campus, Brazil, 1998.

12. According to the Institute of World Resources, tropical forests are being destroyed worldwide at a rate of 0.8 per cent each year. Over the last decade a total of 1.54 million square kilometres have gone—equivalent in area to three Frances. (El Espectador, Colombia, 23 December, 1998).

13. Op. cit. 10.

14. Jose A. Lutzenberger. The climatic effects of tile destruction of the rainforests. FoE campaign, Dec 4, 1988. An update, December, 1998.

15. Victor Menotti, Globalization and the Acceleration of Forest Destruction since Rio, *The Ecologist*, Vol. 28, No. 6, Nov/Dec, 1998.

Sustainable Forest Management Is an Effective Conservation Tool

Joshua C. Dickinson III

Joshua C. Dickinson III is the executive director of the Forest Management Trust, an organization that promotes sustainable management of forests.

Sustainable Forest Management (SFM), a relatively new conservation method, attempts to create a balance between commercial logging and preservation of the rain forest through certification of sustainable forest operations. The Forest Stewardship Council (FSC), the leading certification organization, accredits other organizations that in turn offer independent certification of forest operations. Certification allows some "rainforest-friendly" logging to take place in certain areas of the rain forest that have been certified by the FSC. In addition, FSC certification enables consumers to feel at ease knowing they are purchasing forest products that were produced in ways that did not harm the forest. The FSC is supported by environmental advocates who see certification as a tool for conserving the rain forest outside of protected areas. Social activists see certification as a means of strengthening community-based forestry and increasing the economic benefits of the forests for the poor.

Certification of good forest management represents a new approach in the global effort to sustain our diverse forest ecosystems. Sustainability, a central tenet of certification, is a complex concept, best thought of as a goal to be strived for and redefined in the process. Elements of sustainability with which most would agree include: maintenance of ecological functions and biological diversity of the forest ecosystem; assurance that people who inhabit or work in the forest receive a fair share of the income from forest management; and financial returns from forest management and value-added activities that are profitable and competi-

Reprinted from Joshua C. Dickinson III, "Forest Management as a Tool for Conservation," *Geographical Review*, July 1999; © American Geographical Society. All rights reserved.

tive with conversion of forestland to alternative uses.

Any new idea is likely to be controversial and generate a measure of public uncertainty. This is particularly the case when the idea has major financial implications, advocates a new balance by featuring conservation instead of protection, and signals a shift in emphasis from "command-and-control" regulation of forest use to market-based incentives (Kiker and Putz 1997). The market for certified products is relatively new and small compared with the overall wood trade; there are few brokers, and as yet there are no trade magazines and few product shows. As a result, signals between consumers and producers were at first weak and mixed-evidence of a truly emerging market.

Conscientious consumers are understandably confused. Not many years ago environmental organizations were advocating boycotts on the purchase of tropical woods as a "save-the-rain-forest" measure. In response to pressure, some 200 municipalities in the United States banned the use of tropical woods in public construction. The movement has been even stronger in Europe. Recently, major environmental organizations have reassessed the effect of timber boycotts. Factors considered have included fairness to developing countries and the probability that bans would devalue tropical timber and thus provide additional pressure for conversion of forestland to crops and pasture. The resultant shift to the new, market-based approach has moved quickly.

Not many years ago environmental organizations were advocating boycotts on the purchase of tropical woods as a "save-the-rain-forest" measure.

In 1990 the first forest certification took place, with a teak plantation in Indonesia certified as well-managed by SmartWood, a program of the New York-based Rainforest Alliance. The Woodworkers' Alliance for Rainforest Protection in the United States proposed the creation of the Forest Stewardship Council (FSC) in 1992; the FSC founding assembly was held in late 1993; and the council began to accredit certifiers in 1995 (Viana and others 1996). Although certification was first conceived as a tool for saving tropical forests, representatives from the tropics were quick to point out that logging practices in temperate and boreal forests are, if anything, more destructive than is logging in tropical forests.

The Forest Stewardship Council

On a global scale the FSC, which is based in Oaxaca, Mexico, continues to be the leading certification organization. Its goals are to promote environmentally responsible, socially beneficial, and economically viable management of forests through the establishment of worldwide standards for good forest management. The FSC accredits organizations that in turn offer independent, third-party certification of forest operations. There are now six accredited certifiers, and at least five more are under review. More than 16 million hectares have been certified in thirty countries (FSC 1999). Certifiers also audit and issue chain-of-custody certificates to added-value processors and retailers to assure that any product sold with an FSC label can be traced back to a well-managed forest. The FSC seeks to have its logo inspire as much confidence among environmentally conscientious consumers as "UL Listed" does among safety-conscious buyers of electrical equipment.

FSC certification of good forest management has four distinguishing characteristics. First, it is voluntary: A forest management operation chooses to engage the services of a certifier and may allow its certificate to lapse at any time. Second, it is performance based: The observed performance in the field is measured against a set of common ecological, social, and economic principles and criteria (FSC 1996). Third, certification is largely market based, with demand driven by a combination of consumers, environmental-activist pressure on retailers, and producer perceptions of future consumer and retailer demand, in addition to individual and corporate decisions that good forest management is the "right thing to do." Fourth, the FSC seeks balance in its approach to sustainable management through a governance structure composed of environmental, social, and economic chambers, each internally balanced in representation from countries of the "North" (developed; temperate, boreal) and of the "South" (developing; tropical).

Within the broad framework of the FSC's principles and criteria, national or regional standards are being developed to address specific ecological, social, and economic conditions in order to provide additional guidance to the certifier. Sweden was the first to have its national standards approved by the FSC. The Bolivian standards have also been approved.

The Forest Management Trust, a not-for-profit corporation registered in Florida,[1] has submitted for final review the regional standards for the southeastern United States, one of the eleven U.S. regions engaged in developing standards. This exercise demonstrated the importance of recognizing regionally distinct cultural, social, economic, and ecological differences within the broader framework of the FSC principles. Forestland owners in the Southeast often perceive certification, though voluntary, as "foreign" interference with their property rights (Parker and others 1999). In the Northeast and Appalachia, concerns relate to efficiency in certifying relatively small woodlots, while in the Northwest old growth and clear-cuts are critical issues. Current information on the overall certification process, principles and criteria, and certifiers is available at the FSC Web site, [http://www.fscoax.org]. Information on certification in the United States is maintained by the FSC-U.S. at [http://www.fscus.org].

Certification cases

FSC certification depends on the validity of three basic premises: that, given a credible claim, most consumers prefer a product from a well-managed, environmentally and socially sustainable forest operation rather than the product of a logger who runs roughshod over the forests and the rights of forest dwellers; that retailers will capitalize on this consumer preference and advertise their stocks of products from well-managed forests; and that, given the right signals, retailers will transmit this demand for products from well-managed forests to their brokers and forest-product suppliers. Market-driven certification has made remarkable strides in strengthening the long and complex value chain between the managed forest and the conscientious consumer. The progress made is evident in the following vignettes:

• Consumers who purchase FSC-certified forest products have their confidence in the validity of labeling claims reinforced by having access to reports from independent certifiers. In more practical terms, consumers can rely on the endorsement of forest management certification by widely known environmental organizations, including the World Wildlife Fund (WWF), Greenpeace, the Sierra Club, and the Natural Resources Defense Council.

• Certified forest management operations receive public recognition as good environmental citizens. Regulatory agencies can assume that a firm is obeying the law—unless there is overt evidence to the contrary—because FSC principles require that all laws relating to the environmental and social aspects of a firm's forest operation be obeyed, whether effectively enforced or not. Performance is audited annually by the certifier.

• Certified operations receive the tangible reward of access to markets that are open only to certified products. This is nowhere more evident than in Europe, where the WWF has led in the formation of buyers' groups that are pledged to purchase certified products (WWF 1999). In Great Britain, B&Q, a leading home-improvement retailer, has become a major purchaser of certified products and will purchase them exclusively beginning in the year 2000.

Certified forest management operations receive public recognition as good environmental citizens.

• In a 9 March 1999 press release, Home Depot, a member of the U.S. Certified Forest Products Council, announced its endorsement of "independent, third party forest certification." Given the massive demand that this $30 billion company is capable of generating, it will take several years for certified producers to bring the requisite forest area under certified management. Home Depot has recently hired the president of the Scandinavian furniture manufacturer IKEA to head its international expansion program. This move has the potential for creating national and regional markets for certified products outside North America.

• Insurers and financial organizations are becoming cautious in dealings with firms that cannot document their performance in forest management due to the potential for legal suits and bad publicity. The Overseas Private Investment Corporation (OPIC) requires that any U.S. firm seeking loan guarantees or financing for forest extraction acquire and maintain independent certification of its forest management by an "organization accredited by an international accreditation body (such as the Forest Stewardship Council)" (OPIC 1998). The Andean Development Corporation requires that loan applicants for forestry projects be FSC certified.

• The World Bank–WWF Alliance for Forest Conservation and Sustainable Use was launched in 1997 with the ambitious goals of bringing an additional 50 million hectares of forestland under effective protection and bringing 200 million hectares of forest under independently certified management. The numbers of hectares are less relevant than are the implications of the policy position taken by the World Bank, an organization not noted for early endorsement of "radical" environmental schemes. This is evidence that certification has become a mainstream issue.

Advocacy of FSC certification is a delicate balancing act among environmental, social, and economic interests.

• British Columbia–based McMillan Bloedel, one of North America's larger timber companies, has broken ranks with a B.C. industry alliance formed to resist pressures from the environmental community and is seeking FSC certification (Hayward 1998). McMillan Bloedel is the first major firm to break ranks with the heretofore solid bloc of large Canadian and U.S. firms and to join smaller certified companies, such as the Collins Pine Company in California and Seven Islands Land Company in Maine. The subsequent acquisition of the Canadian company by Weyerhaeuser, in June 1999, injects a new dynamic, given the U.S. firm's past lack of enthusiasm for the FSC. The most notable European firm to become certified is Sweden's Assi Doman.

• When the Bolivia Sustainable Forestry project was designed in 1994, the FSC had been in existence for less than a year. As something of a gamble, the designers of the project specified that its assistance to forest enterprises would be conditional on the companies and communities making a commitment to seek certification. The designers were aware that the FSC principles and criteria were more demanding and had the potential for greater international credibility than did the environmental regulations of the U.S. Agency for International Development, the funding agency. Four years later, more than 1 million hectares either have been certified or are in the process of becoming so (Nittler and Nash 1999).

Green rewards

Advocacy of FSC certification is a delicate balancing act among environmental, social, and economic interests. The dominant actors have been the environmental community, which sees certification as a tool for conserving forest ecosystems outside protected areas. Environmental advocates are supported, particularly in developing countries, by social activists who see certified management primarily as a means of strengthening community-based forestry and reinforcing tenure claims and secondarily as a means of assuring workers' and forest dwellers' rights and increasing economic benefits for the poor from large concessionaires' forest operations. Less effectively represented, but critical to the success of the balancing act, are commercial timber interests, which must find certified management more attractive than conventional logging. If timber companies fail to make money in certified forestry, the whole elaborate construct falls apart.

Certification has costs for training, forest and ecological inventories, preparation of management plans, and maintenance of records, as well as certification assessment and annual audits. There must be a continuing dialog between business interests in the economic chamber and the environmental and social chambers to assure that a balance is maintained between the ideal and the economically feasible. Ironically, the magnitude of market share and green premiums that attract forest enterprises to certification depends on the extent to which their operations can be credibly differentiated from business-as-usual logging. The credibility and magnitude of the differentiation is what energizes the environmental and social organizations that educate consumers and directly influence forest-product purchasing decisions by retailers. Some organizations effectively use the carrot: the WWF organizes buyers' groups and promotes the benefits of certification. Other organizations use negative publicity about environmental behavior to convince producers and retailers of the virtues of certification. Greenpeace and the Rainforest Action Network have been particularly effective stick wielders.

Joint ventures

Proponents of participation in forestry by peasant and indigenous communities see certification as a tool for fostering economic development and promoting alternatives to deforestation for agriculture. Some 2 million hectares of community and indigenous forest operations have been certified in tropical countries, including five communities in the Peten of Guatemala in mid-1998. Should social activists and consumers expect to see certified products from community forests at Home Depot? Doors from Portico's industrial operation in Costa Rica are there. However, the prospects for communities entering the certified market are poor, so poor that it is naive to promote certification without major changes in the approach.

To ensure the successful participation of communities in the certified market, the Forest Management Trust proposes that communities form joint ventures with successful private-sector forest enterprises. Such ventures stand to benefit both partners. Certified joint ventures offer the private sector reliable access to raw materials while assuring communities equitable treatment in business dealings. The issue of access is significant where indigenous groups have gained control over extensive areas of forest, as has been the case in Bolivia and Canada. Competent private-sector firms have what the communities and their supporting nongovernmental organizations (NGOs) lack—the technology, capital, contacts, and business acumen to function in the market. Of course, this requires that the community's supporting expatriate and local NGOs play a markedly different role in community forest projects from the role they played in the past. The new role calls for NGOs to empower communities by training them to deal with an unaltruistic business partner. The NGO serves as a watchdog to help assure that both partners adhere to the social, economic, and environmental conditions imposed (voluntarily) by certification. This arrangement has the potential for reducing the NGOs costs of involvement and the level of dependency created while increasing the probability that the forest operation will be sustainable and profitable— for both partners.

Opposition to forest management certification

FSC certification has earned the opposition of those interests that are most threatened by its success in the short run. Most vociferous in their complaints about the alleged environmental bias of the FSC, the unprofitability of certified forestry, and the threat to free trade posed by voluntary certification are the American Forest & Paper Association and the International Wood Products Association. These groups rightfully fear voluntary, independent certification because it gives consumers the power to differentiate among otherwise identical products according to the forest management practices of the supplier. In the longer term, the commitment of the certification movement to the sustainability of forest management and, specifically, the requirement that harvest volume equal regeneration assures the future of the forest industry. Individual companies are starting to break ranks as they see opportunities to gain market share.

Opposition to forest management as a strategy for maintaining forest ecosystems, with certification as a core element, has arisen within the conservation community itself—a veritable circular firing squad of organizations with a common goal but with different approaches (Dickinson, Dickinson, and Putz 1996). Some groups simply oppose logging altogether; others seek bans on logging in tropical rain forests or in old-growth forests. The Sierra Club supports certification of private forestlands in the United States but vehemently opposes certification on federal lands because they are continuing advocates of legislation before Congress, which would prohibit commercial logging in national forests.

Opposing views must be heard, evaluated, and addressed as needed. Forest industry opposition will fade as individual companies find that an expanded market justifies their becoming certified producers or value-added processors of certified products. Of paramount importance is the credibility of certified forest management within the scientific community and with conscientious decision makers, both corporate and individual. Scientific credibility requires continuing research to refine and improve the ecological basis for certifiable forest management (Putt and Viana 1996). The level of public awareness must be raised and translated into pressure to stock more products from certified, well-managed forests.

The future of forest management certification

What is the future of forest management certification? Certification is only a tool. The more relevant question is: Does society, in rich and poor countries alike, find value in maintaining forest ecosystems outside parks that have a dual function of generating income while maintaining biological diversity? Increasing efforts by environmental organizations to educate the public and to pressure the forest sector to adopt certified good-management practices are needed. The recent decisions by Home Depot and IKEA to support certification are two of the most important breakthroughs, assuming that the certified production base can be expanded while maintaining the credibility of the FSC trademark. In fact, the market is already lucrative enough to have attracted its share of charlatans. Consumers must ask: Does the dealer hold FSC chain-of custody certification? Does the product advertisement identify an FSC-accredited certifier?

You, the reader of this, are part of the answer. Your willingness to seek out and purchase certified forest products will send a signal back to the producer in Georgia or Bolivia that practicing good forest management pays.

Notes

1. The purpose of the Forest Management Trust, [http://www.foresttrust.org], is to promote sustainable management of forests for timber and nontimber products and services. Activities have been funded by private foundations, including the MacArthur Foundation and the Moriah Fund, the U.S. Agency for International Development, and the U.S. Forest Service.

References

Dickinson, M.B., J.C. Dickinson, and F. E. Putz. 1996. Natural Forest Management as a Conservation Tool in the Tropics: Divergent Views on Possibilities and Alternatives. *Commonwealth Forestry Review* 4 (75): 309–15.

FSC [Forest Stewardship Council]. 1996. Forest Stewardship Council Principles and Criteria for Forest Management. Oaxaca, Mexico: Forest Stewardship Council. Mimeographed. 1999. [http://www.fscoax.org].

Hayward, J. 1998. Certifying Industrial Forestry in B.C. Understory [*Journal of the Certified Forest Products Council*] 4 (8):1, 6–9.

Kiker, C.F., and F.E. Putz. 1997. Ecological Certification of Forest Products: Economic Challenges. *Ecological Economics* ao (1): 37–51.

Nittler, J.B., and D.W. Nash. 1999. The Certification Model for Forestry in Bolivia. *Journal of Forestry* 97 (3): 32–36.

OPIC [Overseas Private Investment Corporation]. 1998. Request for Comments on Draft Environmental Handbook. Federal Register, 25 February, 9696–9709.

Parker, J.K., V.E. Sturtevant, M.A. Shannon, W.R. Burch Jr., J.M. Grove, J.C. Ingersoll, and L. Sagel. 1999. Some Contributions of Social Theory to Ecosystem Management. In *Ecological Stewardship: A Common Reference for Ecosystem Management* edited by N.C. Johnson, A.J. Malk, W.T. Sexton, and R. Szaro, 245–277. Oxford: Elsevier Science.

Putz, F. E., and V. Viana. 1996. Biological Challenges for Certification of Tropical Timber. *Biotropica* 3 (28): 323–30.

Viana, V.M., J. Ervin, R.Z. Donovan, C. Elliott, and H. Gholz, eds. 1996. Certification of Forest Products: Issues and Perspectives. Washington, D.C.: Island Press.

WWF [World Wildlife Fund]. 1999. WWF's Global Forests and Trade Initiative News, Spring.

10
Sustainable Forest Management May Not Be Effective

Laura Tangley

Laura Tangley is a writer for U.S. News & World Report *and coauthor of* Trees of Life: Saving Tropical Forests and Their Biological Wealth.

Sustainable logging, also known as sustainable forest management (SFM), is a conservation tool that allows carefully supervised logging in certain areas of the rain forests. The idea behind SFM is to allow "rainforest-friendly" logging as a compromise between all-out protection and total destruction of the rain forest. The slogan for SFM is "Buy *good wood* and help save the rain forest." However, new evidence shows that sustainable harvests may damage rain forests and their ecosystems more than standard logging practices. In addition, environmental and development organizations have invested hundreds of millions of dollars into sustainable forestry, but only a small proportion of tropical forests are managed sustainably.

Save the rain forest: Buy "good wood." That advice, preached by conservationists for over a decade, may turn out to be as controversial as logging itself.

In spring 1998, the World Bank pledged to help establish 500 million acres of "sustainable" forestry projects by 2005, half of them in the tropics. The organization also is considering lifting a seven-year-old ban on funding logging in virgin tropical forests. But the bank, the largest funder of forestry projects worldwide, is acting just as scientific evidence mounts that sustainable harvests may damage tropical forests and their wealth of biodiversity more than standard logging practices. Not only does the strategy appear to be uneconomical, it may wreak more havoc—and for longer—than the usual method.

Conventional logging is done differently in the tropics than in the temperate zone. Unlike temperate forests, which are relatively uniform,

Reprinted from Laura Tangley, "Sustainable Logging Proves Unsupportable," *U.S. News & World Report*, June 29, 1998, with permission. © 1998, U.S. News & World Report. Web site: www.usnews.com.

tropical forests, which supply about one fifth of the world's industrial timber, house hundreds of different tree species, and only a few have commercial value. Because of that, tropical forests aren't clear-cut. Yet loggers, who harvest trees from millions of acres of tropical forest each year, still do considerable damage. While cutting target trees, lumbermen damage dozens of neighboring trees, disturbing plant and animal life. They also build roads that open areas to land-hungry farmers, who clear trees to grow crops or to raise cattle.

Seductive solution

The logic behind sustainable forest management is seductive: Provide a long-term economic stake in the forest through a permanent supply of carefully harvested, regenerating timber, and users would harvest trees more carefully. In addition, tropical nations could earn money from forests, providing an economic incentive to stop clearing land for agriculture, the No. 1 reason tropical forests are destroyed. Environmental and development organizations have poured hundreds of millions of dollars into sustainable forestry, but these investments have produced few results. In June 1998 in *Science*, Ian Bowles and colleagues from Conservation International, a U.S.-based environmental organization, calculate that, outside plantations, less than 0.02 percent of the world's tropical forests are managed sustainably for timber.

The major barrier to sustainable forestry's success is basic economics. "Reaping a one-time harvest of ancient trees today is simply more profitable than managing for future harvests," writes Bowles, citing studies concluding that "unsustainable" logging yields profits 20 percent to 450 percent higher than do sustainable methods. So far, markets for "good wood," environmentally friendly products, have not made it profitable, either. Most of these markets are in the United States and Europe, which import only about 5 percent of all tropical timber. A policy shift at the World Bank could radically change the picture by subsidizing sustainable logging in huge new tracts.

Reaping a one-time harvest of ancient trees today is simply more profitable than managing for future harvests.

The first scientists to go public with their doubts about sustainable logging uncovered the problems during a project designed to make the strategy work better. In 1991, Raymond Gullison, a tropical ecologist then at Princeton University, and Richard Rice, a resource economist for Conservation International, launched a four-year study of Bolivia's Chimanes rain forest, chosen by the International Tropical Timber Organization as a model site for sustainable mahogany harvests. Midway through the study, the researchers concluded that the project not only was economically unsound but also could do the forest more harm than good. They found that ensuring regrowth of mahogany—which naturally regenerates only after large disturbances such as fire—would require thinning so much other vegetation that biodiversity would be threatened.

Two studies in June 1998's *Conservation Biology* report that even the selective logging required under sustainable forestry can reduce tropical biodiversity. One, which looked at logging's effects on birds on the Indonesian island of Seram, discovered that even lightly logged forests had fewer species than unlogged forests (57 versus 73). The second found that harvesting a single tree species from a Brazilian rain forest created artificial gaps that may boost the number of large, heat-loving lizards, voracious predators that eat smaller lizards and frogs. The longer such disturbances continue—indefinitely in the case of sustainable logging—the worse might be the damage. "We should not pretend that sustainable timber production is compatible with sustainable biodiversity conservation," says Peter Ashton, a tropical-forest ecologist at Harvard University.

The best hope

Proponents of sustainable forestry say such criticism threatens a conservation strategy that, although imperfect, represents the best realistic hope for humans and forests to coexist. "Like it or not, the overwhelming majority of tropical forests will be subject to timber extraction," says Bruce Cabarle, director of the World Wildlife Fund's Global Forest Program. Michael Kiernan, senior forestry specialist at the World Bank, believes the forest studied by Rice and Gullison "is a unique situation that does not apply across the board." He says that in less remote forests, where timber transport is cheaper, loggers operating conventionally may harvest several species, rather than just one, and do far more damage.

Some scientists who question sustainable forestry's usefulness believe it can work under some circumstances. Biologists Peter Frumhoff of the Union of Concerned Scientists and Elizabeth Losos of the Smithsonian Institution's Center for Tropical Forest Science say that sustainable management could protect tropical forests that are not a top priority for conservation, but only if the forests are threatened by clear-cutting for agriculture and either local law or economics dictate that harvests will truly be regulated. Few places in the world meet those criteria.

Radical alternative

For forests like Chimanes, Gullison and Rice propose a radical alternative: Let loggers come in and take the few valuable trees quickly, rather than encouraging them to work in the forest for many years. Once those trees are gone, they say, governments or conservation organizations could purchase the land cheaply and make it a protected area. As an example, Rice points to a project in Bolivia, in which the Nature Conservancy coordinated a plan to buy out loggers' rights to a 1.5 million-acre rain forest that the government then added to a national park. The land cost $1.6 million but would have cost 20 times that much if it had not been lightly logged for mahogany. Rice compares the $1.6 million investment to millions spent trying to make logging in Chimanes sustainable, a project that "hasn't produced anything so far."

11

Brazilians Have Begun to Fight to Save Their Rain Forest

Diana Alves

Diana Alves is a Brazilian journalist specializing in the environment.

International and foreign organizations have long fought to preserve the Amazon rain forest, but now for the first time the Brazilian people are leading their own crusade to save the forest. Brazilian public opinion has switched from supporting the forest trade to fighting against it as a result of the economic disaster of unregulated logging. For example, in 2000, popular protest contributed to the defeat of legislation that would have greatly increased the number of trees that could be legally felled in the Amazon region.

B razil's ecologists and rural landowners will remember 2000 as the year of confrontation. Both wanted to decide the future of the world's biggest biological reserve. A mass petition, protest demonstration and torrent of 20,000 e-mail messages supported the country's nongovernmental organizations (NGOs) and blocked an amendment to the national forestry regulations that would have increased by a quarter the number of trees that could be legally felled in the Amazon region, which lost an estimated 532,000 sq km of forest between 1978 and 1997.

Brazilian support

At the height of the confrontation, a public opinion poll showed that 88 percent of the electorate would vote against parliamentary candidates who backed the amendment. Ninety-three percent of those questioned said protecting the environment did not hinder the country's development, while 90 percent believed that cutting down more trees would not help reduce hunger. Even more important was the finding that in a country where few people read newspapers, 63 percent said they had closely followed the debate, mostly through radio and television reports.

Reprinted from Diana Alves, "Brazil Turns Its Back on the Amazon Trade," *The Unesco Courier*, November 2000.

The financial press was firmly against the amendment too. "There is not a single argument that can justify this disastrous measure," said the influential newspaper *Gazeta Mercantil.* "Brazil has plenty of fertile land. There are more than 100 million hectares of unused land alone in the sertao," the scrubland that covers a quarter of the country. Amazonia has lost 60 percent of its original vegetation through the spread of soybean farming and especially pasture land for cattle.

Another major Brazilian newspaper, *O Estado de Sao Paulo,* summed up the worries about the future with a headline that asked: "What kind of air are we going to breathe?" The popularity of the ecologists' campaign could be seen through the fact that characters in the cartoon strip *Monica,* which appears in dozens of newspapers, were dressed in mourning clothes as a sign of protest.

Leading their own crusade

"For the first time Brazilian society is reacting, organizing itself and getting results through a major campaign that started inside the country," says Eduardo Martins, until 2000 head of the federal environment agency, IBAMA. "In Amazonia, the proposed amendment was denounced by sectors that have never stirred before, such as the middle class and the local media," declares biologist Adalberto Verissimo, a researcher with the Institute of People and the Environment in Amazonia, IMAZON, one of the region's most respected NGOs. "Everyone understood that a public resource was about to be destroyed without generating any kind of development."

For the first time Brazilian society is reacting, organizing itself and getting results through a major campaign that started inside the country.

Brazilian public opinion, which is now in tune with what many international bodies and organizations have been advocating for years, has switched as a result of the economic disaster of unregulated logging. Most of the destroyed forest areas have become pasture land or soybean, palm, coffee and black pepper plantations. These foreign crops, which are ill-suited to poor soil and heavy rains, have had a hard time growing over two-thirds of the deforested area. Half the 20 million hectares of pasture are also in a miserable state.

Low yields made farmers look for new land, causing deforestation to increase year after year—always in vain, however, because 78 percent of the soil was too acidic and had little natural fertility. Along with this vicious circle, there were transport problems. It takes several days by river to get from the ranches deep in the jungle to a port from where crops can be sent out to domestic and foreign markets.

So although 14 percent of Amazonia's virgin forest has been destroyed, it is still a poor area and its 20 million inhabitants—three-quarters of whom live in towns—only produce seven percent of the country's GDP [gross domestic product]. Per capita income there is below the national average, while the region's main export, Brazil nuts, is only worth about

$3 million, far behind the $230 million earned from the urban production of syrups for soft drinks.

The waste of sawmills and the defiance of loggers

A recent survey carried out by IMAZON for the World Bank showed why farming in the region is so difficult. It noted that 18 percent of the Brazilian part of the Amazon was given over to cattle-raising. That area, in the far south of the Amazon, is the most deforested part and has a low annual rainfall of 1,800 mm. To the north is a mixed zone that has a little more rain and where farming is still feasible, despite a host of insects and plant diseases. In the remaining 45 percent of Brazilian Amazonia, where heavy rain falls each day, the only viable large-scale economic activity is forestry. "Here and in the mixed zone, logging is as profitable as agriculture," says Verissimo, one of the experts involved in the survey, "That shows forestry is the best thing for Amazonia."

But the timber industry has not managed to make use of this natural resource without destroying it. Nearly three years ago a European Commission report blamed the industry for 72 percent of deforestation, and said its activities were much more harmful to the forests than felling by farmers or ranchers. The sawmills also waste an enormous amount of timber, sometimes as much as two-thirds of the trees felled. Even worse, most timber firms do not obey the law. "The strategic affairs ministry says about 80 percent of the timber is illegally chopped down in the region and forest management schemes are mostly ignored," says a survey put together by Greenpeace.

Brazil contains the planet's richest biodiversity and the widest range of plant species.

What are these schemes? First, there is the battle to keep current forestry regulations on the books and strictly enforce them. During the 1960s, each landowner was required to preserve 50 percent of the forests on his land. As deforestation sped up, parliament decreed in 1996 that 80 percent must be preserved. President Fernando Henrique Cardoso sided with the ecologists, saying that "forestry regulations are needed to ensure the survival of Amazonia, which belongs to Brazilians but also to humanity as a whole."

A haven for biodiversity is the last farming frontier

Brazil contains the planet's richest biodiversity and the widest range of plant species. A sixth of all the world's birds live there, an eighth of all amphibians, one in every 11 mammals and a 15th of the world's reptiles. Five thousand different kinds of trees grow in the Amazon, against North America's 650.

Another scheme currently on the books is the Pilot Programme to Preserve Tropical Forests, funded by the G7 [group of seven industrialized] countries, the European Union and the Brazilian government, which have together contributed $280 million to support sustainable use of the forests. The programme is the biggest multilateral investment in the environment ever made in a single country.

As well as these schemes, there is the Amazon Region Protected Areas Programme, backed by Brazil, the World Bank and other international bodies, such as the World Wildlife Fund and the World Bank Forest Alliance Programme. It aims to convert 10 percent of Amazonia into protected areas. Twelve million hectares are already protected, and the goal is to increase that to 37 million hectares—an area the size of Germany.

All these conservation measures are opposed in varying degrees by Amazonian landowners, who see the region's 5.1 million sq kms as the last agricultural frontier, with unlimited possibilities for growth. They say society owes them something for having stopped felling on part of their lands to help safeguard the environment, and are demanding monetary compensation.

It would seem hard to ignore Brazilian public opinion, which now broadly agrees with arguments that until recently were dismissed as unpatriotic and slavish to foreign interests.

An all-party parliamentary commission, headed by the pro-government centre-right deputy Mosir Micheletto, tabled a draft law at the end of 1999 to allow a very flexible interpretation of the forestry regulations. Micheletto's bill stipulated that half of Amazonia's ranchland should remain uncleared, but that Amazonian state governments would be able to grant special logging concessions on a case by case basis. Estates of less than 25 hectares, meanwhile, would be exempted from all conservation regulations.

During a demonstration in favour of the new proposal, 600 members of the National Agricultural Federation made a nationalistic protest against what they called "the harmful interference of national and foreign ecological organizations in drafting punitive laws which hinder national development."

Environment Minister Jose Sarney Filho, the National Environment Council (CONAMA) and the NGOs responded by pointing out the need to continue preserving 80 percent of the Amazonian forest. For six months, they organized public debates all over Brazil.

Battles among the region's shareholders

The ecologists overwhelmingly support the government's stand. Their main criticism is that the scrubland areas of the Amazon must also be safeguarded, since—contrary to most people's beliefs—jungle is not the only native vegetation in the Amazon. Environmental NGOs say it is not enough to leave only 35 percent of the ranchland in this ecosystem untouched, as CONAMA proposes, let alone descend to the 20 percent threshold in the Micheletto proposal. Either way, it would seem hard to ignore Brazilian public opinion, which now broadly agrees with arguments that until recently were dismissed as unpatriotic and slavish to foreign interests.

Organizations to Contact

The editors have compiled the following list of organizations concerned with the issues debated in this book. The descriptions are derived from materials provided by the organizations. All have publications or information available for interested readers. The list was compiled on the date of publication of the present volume; the information provided here may change. Be aware that many organizations take several weeks or longer to respond to inquiries, so allow as much time as possible.

Canadian Nature Federation
1 Nicholas St., Suite 606, Ottawa, ON K1N 7B7 Canada
(800) 267-4088 • (613) 562-3447
e-mail: cnf@cnf.ca • website: www.cnf.ca/

The federation seeks to protect the Canadian landscape through a two-pronged strategy of establishing protected wilderness areas and promoting ecologically sound environmental management policies. It implements several programs focusing on conservation of wildlands, habitat, and ancient forests. It publishes the magazine *Nature Canada* and the quarterly newsletter *Nature Alert.*

Competitive Enterprise Institute (CEI)
1001 Connecticut Ave., NW, Suite 1250, Washington, DC 20036
(202) 331-1010 • fax: (202) 331-0640
e-mail: info@cei.org • website: www.cei.org

CEI encourages the use of private incentives and property rights to protect the environment. It advocates removing governmental barriers in order to establish a system in which the private sector would be responsible for the environment. CEI publications include the monthly newsletter *CEI Update,* the book *The True State of the Planet,* and the report *The World's Forests: Conflicting Signals.*

Environmental Defense Fund
257 Park Ave., South, New York, NY 10010
(212) 505-2100 • fax: (212) 505-2375
e-mail: contact@environmentaldefense.org • website: www.edf.org

The fund is a public interest organization of lawyers, scientists, and economists dedicated to the protection and improvement of environmental quality and public health. It publishes the bimonthly *EDF Letter* and the reports *Fires in the Amazon* and *Murder, Mahogany, and Mayhem: The Tropical Timber Trade.*

Forest Action Network (FAN)
Box 625, Bella Coola, BC V0T 1C0 Canada
(250) 799-5800 • fax: (250) 799-5830
e-mail: fanbc@envirolink.org • website: www.fanweb.org

FAN is a grassroots organization with a network of over five hundred forest activists and twenty-two organizations throughout British Columbia, North

America, and Europe. FAN has traditionally relied on widely publicized direct action to stop destructive logging and to create media opportunities to effectively articulate important ecological principles. It publishes news reports on FAN activities and reports such as *Forests in Trust: A Backgrounder.*

Forest Alliance of British Columbia
PO Box 49312, 1055 Dunsmuir St.,Vancouver, BC V7X 1L3 Canada
(604) 685-7507 • (800) 567-TREE • fax: (604) 685-5373
website: www.forest.org

The Forest Alliance is a coalition of citizens whose common concern is to protect British Columbia's forest environment and forest-based economy. Members seek to combine environmental protection with economic stability in the use of forest resources, and they work to keep the public informed of the current state of British Columbia's forests and forestry practices. The Forest Alliance's publications include the journal *Choices* and the reports *Forests on the Line* and *Tropical and Temperate Rainforests.*

Global Warming International Center (GWIC)
International Headquarters
22W381 75th St., Naperville, IL 60565-9245
(630) 910-1551 • fax: (630) 910-1561
e-mail: syshen@magsinet.net
website: www2.msstate.edu/~krreddy/glowar/glowar.html

The GWIC is an international body that disseminates information concerning global warming science and policy. It serves both governmental and nongovernmental organizations as well as industries in more than one hundred countries. The center sponsors research on global warming and its mitigation. It publishes the quarterly newsletter *World Resource Review.*

Greenpeace USA
1436 U St., NW, Washington, DC 20009
(202) 462-1177 • fax: (202) 462-4507
website: www.greenpeaceusa.org

Affiliated with Greenpeace International, this organization consists of conservationists who believe that verbal protests against environmental threats are inadequate and advocate action through nonviolent confrontation. Greenpeace's many concerns include preserving biodiversity and preventing pollution. It publishes *Greenpeace Magazine* as well as books and reports, including *Principles and Guidelines for Ecologically Responsible Forest Use.*

Heritage Foundation
214 Massachusetts Ave., NE, Washington, DC 20002-4999
(202) 546-4400 • fax: (202) 546-8328
e-mail: info@heritage.org • website: www.heritage.org

The Heritage Foundation is a conservative think tank that supports free enterprise and limited government in environmental matters. Its publications, such as the quarterly magazine *Policy Review* and the occasional papers *Heritage Talking Points,* include studies on environmental regulations and government policies.

International Society of Tropical Foresters (ISTF)
5400 Grosvenor Ln., Bethesda, MD 20814
(301) 897-8720 • fax: (301) 897-3690
e-mail: istf@igc.org • website: www.cof.orst.edu/org/istf

The ISTF strives to develop and promote ecologically sound methods of managing and harvesting the world's tropical forests. The society provides information and technical knowledge about the effects of deforestation on agriculture, forestry, industry, and the environment. The ISTF publishes the quarterly newsletter *ISTF News*.

International Wood Products Association (IWPA)
4214 King St., West, Alexandria, VA 22302
(703) 820-6696 • fax: (703) 820-8550
e-mail: info@iwpawood.org • website: www.iwpawood.org

The IWPA is committed to promoting and enhancing trade in the imported wood products industry. Through its Conservation, Utilization, Reforestation, Education (CURE) Program, the IWPA seeks to increase public acceptance and use of wood products and to illustrate the positive role commercial forestry plays in the conservation of the world's tropical forests. It publishes bulletins and the newsletter *IWPA News*.

Rainforest Action Network (RAN)
221 Pine St., Suite 500, San Francisco, CA 94104
(415) 398-4404 • fax: (415) 398-2732
e-mail: rainforest@ran.org • website: www.ran.org

RAN works to preserve the world's rain forests through activism and by addressing the logging and importation of tropical timber, cattle ranching in rain forests, and the rights of indigenous rain forest peoples. It also seeks to educate the public about the environmental effects of tropical hardwood logging. RAN's publications include the monthly bulletin *Action Report* and the semiannual *World Rainforest Report*.

Rainforest Alliance
65 Bleecker St., New York, NY 10012
(212) 677-1900 • fax: (212) 677-2187
e-mail: canopy@ra.org • website: www.rainforest-alliance.org

The alliance is composed of individuals concerned with the conservation of tropical forests. Its members strive to expand awareness of the role the United States plays in the fate of tropical forests and to develop and promote sound alternatives to tropical deforestation. The alliance publishes the bimonthly newsletter *Canopy*.

Rainforest Conservation Fund
2036 N. Clark St., Suite 233, Chicago, IL 60614
(773) 975-7517
e-mail: rcf@interaccess.com • website: www.rainforestconservation.org

The Rainforest Conservation Fund is a volunteer organization dedicated to preserving the world's tropical forests. Its main project focuses on the rain forest preserve Reserva Comunal Tamshiyacu-Tahuayo in the Peruvian Amazon. The fund works with the local people to develop preservation programs and to maintain the integrity of the forest. Articles and field reports published by the fund include *The Importance of Blackwater Rivers as an Ecosystem* and *Why the Tahuayo River?*

Reason Foundation
3415 S. Sepulveda Blvd., Suite 400, Los Angeles, CA 90034-6064
(310) 391-2245 • fax: (310) 391-4395
e-mail: cato@ix.netcom.com • website: www.reason.org

The Reason Foundation is a national public policy research organization. It specializes in a variety of policy areas, including the environment, education, and privatization. The foundation publishes the monthly magazine *Reason* and the book *Global Warming: The Greenhouse, Whitehouse, and Poorhouse Effect.*

Sierra Club
85 Second St., 2nd Floor, San Francisco, CA 94105
(415) 977-5500 • fax: (415) 977-5799
e-mail: information@sierraclub.org • website: www.sierraclub.org

The Sierra Club is a grassroots organization that promotes the protection and conservation of natural resources. It publishes the bimonthly magazine *Sierra,* the monthly Sierra Club activist resource the *Planet,* and several books, including *Into the Amazon: The Struggle for the Rainforest* and *Lessons of the Rainforest.*

World Resources Institute (WRI)
10 G St., NE, Suite 800, Washington, DC 20002
(202) 729-7600 • fax: (202) 729-7610
e-mail: lauralee@wri.org • website: www.wri.org

The WRI conducts policy research on global resources and environmental conditions. It publishes books, reports, and papers; holds briefings, seminars, and conferences; and provides the print and broadcast media with new perspectives and background materials on environmental issues. The institute publishes the books *The Right Climate for Carbon Taxes: Creating Economic Incentives to Protect the Atmosphere* and *The Greenhouse Trap: What We're Doing to the Atmosphere and How We Can Slow Global Warming.*

Worldwatch Institute
1776 Massachusetts Ave., NW, Washington, DC 20036-1904
(202) 452-1999 • fax: (202) 296-7365
e-mail: worldwatch@worldwatch.org • website: www.worldwatch.org

Worldwatch is a research organization that analyzes and focuses attention on global problems, including environmental concerns such as maintaining biodiversity and the relationship between trade and the environment. It compiles the annual *State of the World* anthology and publishes the bimonthly magazine *World Watch* and the Worldwatch Paper Series, which includes *Saving the Forest: What Will It Take?* and *Reforesting the Earth.*

Bibliography

Books

Catherine Caufield — *In the Rainforest*. Chicago: University of Chicago Press, 1991.

Ellen Davis — *Life at the Top: Discoveries in a Tropical Forest Canopy*. Rainforest Pilot Series: Vaughn Publishers, 2000.

Ricardo A. Godoy — *Indians, Markets and Rainforests: Theoretical, Comparative and Quantitative Explorations in the Neotropics*. New York: Columbia University Press, 2001.

Brian Johnson — *Responding to Tropical Deforestation: An Eruption of Crises, an Array of Solutions*. Washington, D.C.: World Wildlife Fund and Conservation Foundation, 1991.

Christopher Joyce — *Earthly Goods: Medicine-Hunting in the Rain Forest*. Boston: Little, Brown, 1994.

Mattias Klum — *Borneo Rainforest*. San Francisco: Chronicle Books, 1998.

Ian McAllister, Karen McAllister, and Cameron Young — *The Great Bear Rainforest: Canada's Forgotten Coast*. San Francisco: Sierra Club Books, 1998.

Kenton Miller and Laura Tangley — *Trees of Life: Saving Tropical Forests and Their Biological Wealth*. Boston: Beacon Press, 1991.

Norman Myers — *The Primary Source: Tropical Forests and Our Future*. New York: Norton, 1992.

Karen Pandell — *Journey Through the Northern Rain Forest*. New York: Penguin Putnam Books for Young Readers, 1999.

Richard Brent Peterson — *Conservations in the Rainforest*. New York: HarperCollins Publishers, 2000.

G.T. Prance, T.H. Brock-Clutton, and D.M. Newberry — *Changes and Disturbance in Tropical Rainforest in South-East Asia*. London: Imperial College Press, 2000.

Larry Pynn — *Last Stands: A Journey through North America's Vanishing Ancient Rainforests*. Corvallis: Oregon State University Press, 2000.

John Vandermeer and Ivette Perfecto — *Breakfast of Biodiversity: The Truth About Rain Forest Destruction*. Oakland, CA: Food First Institute for Food and Development Policy.

Periodicals

Judy Bates — "Troubles in the Rain Forest: British Columbia's Forest Economy in Transition," *Canadian Geographer*, Winter 1999.

76

John J. Berger — "Nine Ways to Save Our Forests," *Sierra*, July/August 1997.

Ian A. Bowles, R.E. Rice, R.A. Mittermeir, and G.A.B. da Fonesca — "Logging and Tropical Forest Conservation," *Science*, June 19, 1998.

Jim Carlton — "Ex-Lumberjacks Lead Fight to Save Tongass Forest," *Wall Street Journal*, December 4, 2000.

Alexander Cockburn — "The Conscience Industry," *Nation*, November 9, 1998.

Wayne Curtis — "The Tiki Wars," *Atlantic Monthly*, February 2001.

Thomas L. Friedman — "Saving the Lost World," *New York Times*, March 31, 2000.

Christopher Hallowell — "Rainforest Pharmacist," *Audubon*, January 1999.

Mochamad Indrawan — "Bitter Chocolate," *Far Eastern Economic Review*, December 21, 2000.

Jen Krill — "Attention Shoppers . . . PA System Takeovers," *Animals' Agenda*, July/August 2000.

Jennifer Lach — "Who's Responsible?" *American Demographics*, December 1999.

Larry Lohmann — "Carbon Con?" *Multinational Monitor*, September 2000.

B.D. Malamud, G. Morein, and D.L. Turcotte — "Forest Fires: An Example of Self-Organized Critical Behavior," *Science*, September 18, 1998.

Quint Newcomer — "The Monteverde Community: A Whole Greater than Its Parts," *Social Education*, March 1999.

Lisa M. Paciulli — "They're Logging Your Rain Forest," *International Wildlife*, July/August 2000.

Doug Peacock — "Land of the Spirit Bear," *Amicus Journal*, Winter 2001.

Fred Pearce — "Going, Going . . . ," *New Scientist*, June 10, 2000.

Paul Rauber — "Heat Wave," *Sierra*, September/October 1997.

David Ruppert — "Brazil's Greens Win Forest Showdown," *World Watch*, September/October 2000.

Kristy Sacato — "Bringing the Rain Forest into a Boardwalk Battle," *New York Times*, January 21, 2001.

Catherine M. Tucker — "Private Versus Common Property Forests: Forest Conditions and Tenure in a Honduran Community, *Human Ecology*, June 1999.

Monica Michael Willis — "Getting Smart in the Rain Forest," *Country Living*, May 2000.

Jim Wyss — "Building a Better Banana," *Amicus Journal*, Winter 2001.

Index